The Playwright's Workbook

The Playwright's Workbook

Jean-Claude van Itallie

APPLAUSE
NEW YORK • LONDON

AN APPLAUSE ORIGINAL
The Playwright's Workbook
by Jean-Claude van Itallie

Library of Congress Cataloging-In-Publication Data

LC Catalog # xx-xxxx

British Library Catalog in Publication Data

A catalogue record for this book is available from the British Library

APPLAUSE BOOKS
211 West 71st Street
New York, NY 10023
Phone (212) 496-7511
Fax: (212) 721-2856

A&C BLACK
Howard Road, Eaton Socon
Huntington, Cambs PE19 3EZ
Phone 0171-242 0946
Fax 0171-831 8478

Distributed in the U.K. and the European Union by A&C Black

First Applause Printing: 1997

Printed in Canada

We're here for such little time on this fair earth, between mystery and mystery. Could we theatre-minded, protean as we are, sense for a moment the melody of our being? And, having sensed it, could we impart it . . . ?

—ROBERT EDMUND JONES

More and more I think it's not a question of new forms or old forms. What matters is to allow what you write to come straight from the heart.

—ANTON CHEKHOV
The Sea Gull

Listening is a far more difficult process than most people imagine. Really to listen . . . is to let go utterly of ourselves, of all the information, all the concepts, all the ideas, and all the prejudices that our heads are stuffed with.

—SOGYAL, RINPOCHE
Tibetan Book of Living and Dying

ACKNOWLEDGMENTS

With profound gratitude to teachers, friends, and students who over the years have contributed to this workbook in one way or another, including:

Joyce Aaron, Stella Adler, Mark Amitin, Robert Anton, Richard Armstrong, Eric Bentley, Glenn Berenbeim, Peter Brook, Robert Brustein, Lillian Butler, Joseph Chaikin, Bill Coco, Emile Conrad-Daoud, Nancy Cooperstein, Robert Chapman, Gordon Davidson, Nick Deutsch, Alvin Epstein, Gwen Fabricant, Kaffe Fassett, Edward Field, Michael Feingold, Merle Feld, Carl Forsman, Mary Frank, Clara Freeman, Sharon Gans, Jean Genet, Richard Giannone, Richard Gilman, Wendy Gimbel, Allen Ginsberg, Joel Gluck, Didi Goldenhar, Peter Goldfarb, Ricky Ian Gordon, Spalding Gray, Jerzi Grotowsky, Cynthia Harris, Jonathan Hart-Makwaia, William G. Hoffman, Morag Hood, Debby Katz, Fred Katz, Roger Klein, Harry Kondoleon, Francoise Kourilsky, Tony Kushner, Rebecca Kutlin, Vicki dello Joio, John Leguizamo, Peggy Ann Lloyd, Leueen MacGrath, Elizabeth Mailer, Kim Mancuso, Shanti Mohling, Wendy MacLeod, Judith Malina, Adam Melnick, Joan Miller, Rob O'Neill, Richard Peaslee, Steven Post, Diane di Prima, David Peters, Carol Fox Prescott, Marianne de Pury, Rosemary Quinn, Gerry Ragni, Gordon Rogoff, Ned Rorem, Birdy Rutkin, Adnan Sarhan, Tony Scheitinger, Daniel Seltzer, Stephanie Sills, Nancy Spanier, Ellen Stewart, David Threlfall, Chogyam Trungpa, Robert Wilson, Glenn Young, David Wolpe, and Lee Worley.

CONTENTS

Workshop Three

Workshop Four

Workshop Five

Workshop Nine

Workshop Ten

Workshop Eleven

Workshop Twelve

Workshop Thirteen

INTRODUCTION

How did I come to write a workbook for playwrights?

Everyone agrees that learning to act requires some practice. But playwrights are often presumed to spring forth full-grown like Athena from the head of Zeus. Playwrights are viewed as artists who must miraculously make something out of nothing. When you are facing a blank page or computer screen, this notion can be daunting. It's more useful for playwrights to consider ourselves vessels or instruments, seismographs, or channels through which energies may flow.

This *Workbook* provides writing exercises for playwrights in the way that acting schools provide acting exercises for actors. When I started teaching, so far as I know, playwriting exercises did not exist. So for many years I invented, applied, and refined my own. While teaching at Princeton I received a publisher's questionnaire asking if I'd use a book on playwriting in my classes if such a book existed. I wrote back saying yes, but only if I wrote it. That was the genesis of this *Workbook*.

Elements covered by the *Workbook* include creating characters, developing story or plot, and writing in the natural rhythms of human speech. Along with theory, the *Workbook* develops the craft of playwriting through a series of exercises. Most of the exercises are executed with writing implements. But the practice and understanding of theater is also a physical and emotional affair. Plays are written from a visceral place as well as from the mind. The idea of the playwright as mere head and hands (with the actor as mindless body) is pernicious. Some of the best playwrights have been actors, including the ancient Greeks and Shakespeare. Performance experience deepens a playwright's knowledge of what is theatrical. So this *Workbook* includes topics not usually associated with writing, such as exercises which require getting up on your feet and using your voice. These exercises are designed to cut through years of mental habits that come between your best intentions and your ability to write effective words.

The *Workbook* doesn't promote any single way to write, or any single style. It explores ways of playwriting through writing games, some based on the work of master playwrights as diverse as Tennessee Williams, Chekhov, Brecht, and Beckett. Suggested readings are included. The *Workbook* does not teach exclusively either "avant-garde" or "realistic" playwriting. Each of the writing exercises becomes a tool in the playwright's toolbox.

You don't need previous experience to use this *Workbook*. If you have some, the *Workbook* may open new horizons. "If your mind is empty, it's always ready for anything, open to everything. In the beginner's mind there are many possibilities, in the expert's mind there are few," Suzuki Roshi says in *Zen Mind, Beginner's Mind*.

The conventional image of the solitary writer is only partly true for a playwright. Choosing to write for the theater means not only choosing to write alone but also choosing to work with others. Knowing that sympathetic colleagues will listen to your writing encourages persistence and makes your writing more grounded. Ideally this *Workbook* assumes meetings of playwriting students working together, doing the assignments between meetings. (The writing games in the *Workbook* are easiest to play when someone reads the rules for each writing section aloud.)

The *Workbook* may, however, also be used by a solitary writer who wants to learn how to write plays and who has the self-discipline to play the writing games alone. If you are working alone, take every opportunity to read aloud what you've written to friends for support and feedback.

Every writer must sometimes assume the important role of listener. When working alone, reading your work aloud into a tape recorder allows you to listen to your work. When working with a group, you have the opportunity to learn through listening to the work of others.

Play the games in the *Workbook* for their own sake. Focussing on process is pleasurable and, paradoxically, the best way to get results. Grimly tensing to write an immortal play only invites failure.

It's best not to look ahead in the *Workbook* at writing games before playing them. The games are given in order of increasing complexity. Played in order and with thoroughness, they will seem easy and yield insights.

In order to cut through hesitation and a general sense of "I can't," writing times are given, along with a general instruction not to stop writing until the time is up. If you write slowly, double the assigned writing time for a game. If, in a longer game you find yourself "on a roll" and want to continue writing for a few more minutes, do so.

While the rules of the games in this *Workbook* are intended to enhance playwriting, keeping them in mind as you write is an acquired skill. As you progress through the exercises, it will become easier.

Don't think of a script as an end in itself, but as a musical score for actors' voices and a blueprint for theatrical action.

Discipline is needed in playwriting, but not anxiety. Anxiety constricts playfulness. Allow your writing to be playful, a game of "listening" to your characters and writing down what you hear.

If you try to conform to an idea of how people *should* speak in plays and impose that idea on your characters, the result will be dull. When you listen to your characters in your mind's ear (and write down what you "hear"), your characters will be strong (and your writing style will be most likely to receive praise). An actor can be inspired by and breathe life into a character when the playwright has "heard" and transcribed that character's unique voice. Of course, dropping assumptions of how people should speak in plays is not easy. Impatience, self-doubt, and anxiety get in the way. Games in this *Workbook* are designed to cut through that anxiety by focussing your attention on the work. Repeat any game you wish, with or without your own variations. The games, intended to stimulate further playwriting, eventually lead you to invent your own games as structures for your own plays.

Be willing to drop preconceptions; work with daring, discipline, and a playful spirit. Training in theater is training to be open and balanced.

Workshop One

DIALOGUE AND THE SPOKEN WORD

PREPARATION: WAYS OF WRITING

In *The Medium is the Message*, Marshall McLuhan says that our minds are shaped by the tools we use. Different physical ways to write have different advantages and disadvantages. Discover which works best for you (and realize that it may change).

Pen (or pencil) and paper slow you down, which may help you to focus. Pen and pencil also allow you to write anywhere — under a tree or in a café or at the beach. (You can write anywhere with a laptop computer, too, but the speed of writing — and therefore the feeling — is different.)

Speaking into a portable tape recorder makes it easier to remain aware of your body and of breathing as you "write," but later you will need to transcribe and edit.

A typewriter requires physical movement, so it too makes use of the body. But using the manual return at the end of each line may make you feel as if you are being forced to repeatedly jump off a cliff. A machine of the factory age, the typewriter seems to have straight-line perfectionist thinking built into it.

The word processor feels more flowing and circular. Material can be easily moved around, without cliffs. On the other hand, the word processor may seduce you into losing touch with your body and breath, becoming exclusively mental, and working too quickly. So, when using one, stretch and stand frequently, look around, remain aware of your physical self breathing in the physical universe.

THE SPACE

Playwrights need a supportive physical environment. Preparing the work space will prepare you to write. Whether working alone or with a group, create an appealing writing environment. If the air is stuffy, open a window. Try to avoid fluorescent lighting (irritating to the ear as well as the eye). When in a group, arrange seating in a circle so that everyone is comfortable and can see everyone else. (Communication is hampered when individuals in a group sit behind tables or large desks.)

➤Just before you start, take a silent moment for yourself.

DIALOGUE: WORKING WITH THE SPOKEN WORD

Playwrights are composers of the spoken word. Spoken words reveal emotion as well as the information they convey, which makes them dramatic. A playwright's pleasure and practice is to listen to spoken words to discover and highlight the feelings hidden in them.

But how to startle and stir people with the same old words everyone speaks all the time? The French playwright Jean Genet said he stopped writing when he'd "twisted and tortured" the French language so much he could twist nothing more from it. Spoken words vibrate in the human body and in space. The tone in which a phrase is spoken can color the space in which it is spoken with emotional meaning. To increase your sense of the power of the spoken word, seize every opportunity to speak your own written words and, by all means, do some acting.

WARM-UP: FITNESS

A healthy body inspires a ready mind. Apart from learning techniques of the craft, a playwright may also enrich her or his playwriting by becoming a more open physical, emotional, and mental instrument of expression. Whenever you can, engage in ongoing practices of physical, emotional, and mental fitness, such as jogging, yoga, good nutrition, singing, dancing, tai chi chuan, painting, playing music, acting, sports, gymnastics, and meditation.

>During any activity, including speaking and writing, try to remain aware of your breathing (without breathing in any special way). This awareness encourages creativity to flow more easily.

Actors usually warm up. Freeing up the body and voice also clears the writer's mind. Here's one warm-up option:

Walk around the space, becoming familiar with all parts of it. Be aware of the ground under you, the space between your head and the ceiling, and the changing space between you, the walls, and any other moving people. As you move, stretch comfortably, letting your body dictate what needs stretching and how. Allow your movements to evolve and change without overly controlling them. Occasionally vary your pace and direction. Be aware of the point about three finger-widths below and an inch behind your navel as a source of energy and breathing. Be aware of your breathing. As you inhale, allow your breath to go to whatever parts of your body feel tense or numb. As you exhale, release the tension or numbness. Allow yourself to make sounds if you wish, but don't force them. Allow your eyes to see what they see, but don't focus your attention on anything. Allow your thoughts to be whatever they are without lending weight or importance to them. Enjoy the walking. You may imagine yourself in the countryside or on a beach. Do this warm-up for about five minutes, then notice how your energy has changed.

PREPARATION: SPEAKING ALOUD

Whenever an exercise in the *Workbook* requires you to speak or read aloud, do it standing up. That commits you to being more physical, which makes you more theatrically effective.

➤Stand where you can see everyone, and where you have a little space to move. Then take three moments to prepare.

➤Take a moment to center yourself. Sense the energy source just below your navel. Be aware of your breathing.

➤Being centered, glance at your listener(s). Include others without abandoning your own center.

➤Start to speak with a step forward. Always involve your body as you speak.

INTRODUCTIONS: IMAGES

Because theater is a succession of imaginative "nows," of present moments, speaking in the present tense is dramatic.

When first getting together with a group of writers (or, if working alone, you can use a tape recorder), try the following theatrical form of introduction.

➤Take the three preparatory steps.

➤Then, *speaking in the present tense* ("I am born in . . .," etc.), give your name and where you were born.

➤Allow the image of an experience you had between childhood and now to occur to you. Speaking in the present tense, briefly relate the experience. Don't offer long explanations about the experience but be specific as to colors, sounds, smells, textures, and tastes.

➤Then, mentally flash on an image of something that occurred today and tell it in the same way.

WRITING WITHOUT STOPPING: BREAKING THE ICE

This exercise introduces the practice of writing without stopping to think, a practice which will be employed throughout the *Workbook*.

When you're ready to start the exercise, leap in and keep writing until time is up. Rather than having to continually glance at a timepiece, it would be best to set a timer. Don't stop and think or edit. Follow the rules and don't worry about the result. Keep as your motto, "Dare to be stupid."

➤Write in the **present tense**.

➤Use **specific images**, not generalizations. (The poet William Butler Yeats said, "The mind that generalizes continually prevents itself from those experiences that would allow it to see and feel deeply.")

➤Filling in the blank, complete the following sentence:

> Last night I dream of a(n) _____.
> This morning as I _____,
> I see_____. Continue writing.

🕐 *Writing time: two minutes.*

➤Now write the following sentence:

> Then, not at all surprised, I _____. (Fill in the blank and continue.)

🕐 *Writing time: three minutes.*

READING ALOUD AND LISTENING

Whether reading aloud to yourself, into a tape recorder, to friends, or to a group of other writers, always read aloud as if yours were the work of someone else, someone whom you admire greatly. (This will bypass any apology in your reading voice which may come from shyness.)

When listening to someone read their work aloud, or when listening to your own tape-recorded voice, listen for what moves you in the writing. (It is what moves you that works theatrically.) As you listen, keep asking yourself: what am I feeling as I hear this?

After you've listened to someone else read their work aloud, tell the writer what, if anything, moved you or made you laugh. Be specific. Something which may seem obvious to you may not be at all obvious to the writer. Avoid abstract and negative criticism. Be generous. Nothing encourages an artist more than heartfelt positive feedback.

OVERHEARD VOICES

The emotional music of everyday speech is the basic cloth from which playwrights fashion plays. How words are spoken reveals emotion through pitch, volume, tone, accent, pausing, repetition, grunts, sounds, and, especially, rhythm. A finely-tuned ear hears the contrast between what a person is saying and how they are saying it. There's often humor in that contrast.

Overheard Voices is a powerful writing tool that hones the playwright's ear. *Overheard Voices* is a continuing assignment. Do it before each workshop in the *Workbook*.

Listening to the music of live voices prepares you to hear your characters' voices instead of unconsciously forcing your characters to speak stereotypically. Each person and each well-drawn character speaks in his or her own unique voice.

ASSIGNMENTS

1. *Overheard Voices*

   As a standing assignment for each workshop, carefully listen to and remember two or three very short spoken exchanges. Listen for these spoken exchanges in a public place (a street, office, airport, cafeteria, grocery store, library, concert hall, etc.)

   Listen for rhythm and music, not merely for information. (While you are "recording" actual words, focus on pitch, volume, hesitations, grunts, pauses, etc.)

   ➤Don't use a recording device other than your mind. (A few written notes are okay.)

   ➤Don't use exchanges in which you yourself take part, exchanges on the telephone, or from the media.

   These exchanges will be used in the next workshop.

2. *Talking with Omitted Parts of Speech*

   As you converse with someone (the topic doesn't matter), agree to omit verbs. For example, if you wish to say, "I'm going home," you might say instead "I to home," or whatever.

   ⏲ *Conversing time: five minutes or longer.*

   This playful and informal conversational game can be played anytime with anyone and with many variations, such as omitting adjectives and/or nouns. It is not a writing game but it can awaken a subtle new awareness of language. (For instance, avoiding "I," "me," and "myself" reveals how language reinforces self-centeredness. Avoiding "you" makes an argument less confrontational.)

For example, now try omitting verbs, pronouns, and proper names. If you wish to say, "I am going home," you might say, "This person to home," or "Must to home."

☉*Conversing time: five minutes or longer.*

3. Suggested Reading

Tennessee Williams' *A Streetcar Named Desire,* Shakespeare's *Hamlet,* and Henrik Ibsen's *A Doll House.*

Workshop Two

BUILDING BLOCKS: WHO, WHERE, WHAT

OVERHEARD VOICES

Visually flash on who was speaking. Press your "mental playback button" and write down the two or three exchanges you overheard. Use dashes, dots, and any other notation to record rhythm, volume, pitch, tone, pauses, grunts, and sighs.

⏱ *Writing time: four minutes, plus one more minute if needed.*

Take three moments to prepare, then read or speak aloud each exchange. It's best to speak these short exchanges from memory. (What's important is to get the rhythm and musicality right, not word for word perfection.)

➤ If you are working alone, speak into a tape recorder. Otherwise, speak to the group.

➤ Don't start by saying where you heard these voices or whose they are.

➤Differentiate between the voices by the way you read, not by naming the speakers.

➤Where you heard a pause, pause (don't *say* "pause").

➤Read with commitment. Do justice to the uniqueness of each voice.

➤Read at a higher volume than you remember hearing the voices. (This compensates for unconscious inhibition.)

➤Avoid forcing words into neat, respectable sentences. Don't rely on stereotypical accents.

➤Take time.

➤Repeat each exchange if you want to do so.

When listening to read back, ask yourself:

➤Are the unique rhythms of each voice distinct?

➤What is happening emotionally under the words?

Laugh when you feel like it. Responsive laughter is welcome. When listeners laugh, *Overheard Voices* have hit the mark. Laughter is often a sign of recognition. *Overheard Voices* may awaken in any hearer the laughter of recognition. When commenting on others' *Overheard Voices*, be supportive.

WHO, WHERE, AND WHAT

"Who," "Where" and "What" are essential building blocks for scenes and need to be determined before you start to write.

"Who" are the characters.

"Where" is the place, the setting.

"What," a more subtle concept, is the dominant image you hold in mind as you write.

Any of "Who," "Where," and "What" can be changed later, after you've stopped writing and before rewriting, but keeping separate the two stages of work — planning and writing — is crucial. First determine the banks of a river and then allow the waters of creativity to flow within those banks. To try determining river banks while the river is flowing creates a frustrating and paralyzing flood. Creating "Who," "Where," and "What" is part of planning before you write.

CREATING THE "WHO": CONFLICT AND CHARACTER

If you feel too close to characters, if they are identical to people you know, you are likely to write them in an overly sentimental or emotional way. If your characters are too distant from you emotionally, if they are pure fabrication, unlike anyone you have ever met, you are likely to make them too cold. The writer Henry James suggests "middle distance." A stereotypical character soon tires the writer and bores the audience. Include in your characters traits of people you know, as well as other traits. Include likeable and unlikeable qualities. Create characters complex and human enough to surprise even their creator.

It is commonly said that for any scene or play to be dramatic, the characters must be in conflict. Conflict in a play has been called "the magic essential." What does that mean for the writer? Should you, before starting to write, invent a goal for each character and an obstacle to that goal? That's a good idea theoretically, but for most writers it is too cerebral an approach to be used exclusively. A complementary method is to imagine characters complex, interesting, profound, and human enough that of course they want something. The specific "something" unfolds when the characters are placed in a situation that interests the playwright. Wanting is (alas) a definition of the human condition, while obstacles to our goals rarely need to be invented. None of us easily achieves our goals, whether it be our own unconscious drives, outside institutions, or fate blocking our way, creating conflict. Conflict in plays is dramatic if the characters are at once unique and familiar, passionate, and, in their own way, articulate. Take for example, Shakespeare's Hamlet. Hamlet wants revenge, but sometimes he wants to kill himself. His conflict is both outer and inner. The play is driven by the complexity and depth of Hamlet's character and by his unique voice.

➤Either alone or with a group of writers (each writer creating a character in turn) imagine a character standing in an empty space in the room. Don't relate the character to any specific setting.

Answer the following questions. Keep notes on what you decide.

➤Who's there in the space?

➤What is the character's gender?

➤What is her or his first name? (To call someone Ms. or Mr. Something keeps the writer and audience at arm's length from that character. Everyone lives at the center of his or her own world.)

➤How old does, say, Jodie appear to be?

➤How does Jodie move — Easily? Hesitantly? Defiantly?

➤Note only what the audience can see or hear when the character first enters. (Jodie may have survived a plane accident when she was ten and earned a doctorate in biochemistry, but if the audience can't know this by seeing her, don't include this information. It's useful to have a fuller biography in mind when writing, but developing one is not what's being done here.)

➤Note specifics that would interest a director and an actor. It's worth noting whether Jodie is attractive. Her race may or may not matter. You may note that Jodie has a commanding air, but to specify her height would limit casting and be disregarded by a director anyway. Note clothes that reveal behavioral and emotional tendencies, ambitions, and idiosyncrasies. Omit unneeded detail. That Jodie wears a bright red jump suit and a single large gold pirate earring may matter, but a list of everything she is wearing is not wanted (a costume designer can improvise from a few specific clues).

➤Make notes on "Who" for at least ten characters.

➤Don't relate the characters to each other.

➤Include characters of different ages (but none less than twelve — anyone younger is tough to cast unless you want an adult playing a child).

EXAMPLES OF "WHO"

✓Amy, 17, jeans, sandals, man's white shirt, attractive, no makeup.

✓Lloyd, 27, neatly tied-back ponytail, well-tailored three-piece suit and conservative tie, running shoes. Sudden twinkles in his eye.

✓Anne-Marie, 18, beautiful, carefully dreadlocked Afro hair, loose blue expensive "ethnic" clothing, thick amber beads, moves regally, has a soft voice.

✓Brad, 21, muscular, black leather jacket, tight jeans, sandals, shoulder-length clean hair and a tee shirt with a dragon on it.

✓Marla, 38, attractive, competent air, pearls, silk blouse, makeup, in a wheelchair.

✓Harry, 40, loose, unkempt clothing and hair, two-day beard, slouches, laid-back with occasional amazing leaps of energy.

✓Howie, 65, straight-backed, green flannel shirt, dirty overalls, reversed baseball cap, talkative.

✓Rose, 45ish, overweight, too many charm bracelets, bright red lipstick, green glasses, loose lime-and-pink flowered dress, talks fast, laughs a lot, has something innocent and open about her.

✓Red Crow, 55, crewcut, potbelly, worn brown sleeveless sweater, loud red tie, huge beautiful silver and turquoise bracelets, authoritative.

✓Laura, 78, white hair neatly pulled back by a large black velvet bow, soft gray jogging suit and shoes, an alert, cheerful look.

CREATING THE "WHERE"

Before you write a scene, see the playing space clearly in your mind. In the stage directions note only the essential details of the space. Usually, and certainly with a familiar public space, a few words of specific description are enough. These specifics will set the emotional atmosphere,and the director and set designer will work from them.

If you want to designate specific stage areas, they are usually noted from the actor's point of view. Juliet in the middle of the stage is "center stage." To her right is "stage right." To her left is "stage left." As she faces the audience, behind her is "upstage," and in front is "downstage."

➤Make a list of at least ten stage spaces you might like to use in a play.

➤Don't relate these "Wheres" to the characters you just created or to each other.

For each space, consider:

➤From what angle is the audience seeing?

➤What time of day or night is it?

➤If exterior, what's the season and weather? If interior, is the space defined principally by vertical or horizontal lines?

➤What colors, textures and objects dominate?

➤Is the space open or cramped?

➤Is the ceiling high or low?

➤Where is the entrance?

➤What is the quality and source of light?

➤Is there anything unexpected about the space or its contents?

➤Don't state obvious or expected details.

EXAMPLES OF "WHERE"

✓Interstate highway "rest area." Mountains. Dusk. Winter.

✓Bedroom. Closed blue curtains. Blue flowered wallpaper. Big bed, chaise lounge, "vanity" dressing table with tufted satin seat and large round mirror.

✓Barn interior. Old wooden walls. Posters of James Dean and Marilyn Monroe. Hay loft above. A rusty, doorless truck serves as furniture.

✓Medical waiting room. No daylight. Salmon-colored molded plastic chairs. Fish tank. Toys on floor. Receptionist's desk.

✓Leafy glade in a wood. Low branches. Mossy stones. Sound of a running brook.

✓Office. Diplomas, awards on walls. Low chair faces the desk.

✓Institutional hallway. Bulletin board with many announcements. One closed door visible.

✓Booth in diner, red plastic and chrome.

✓Living room. Big window opening on autumn trees. Afternoon. Large round cluttered coffee table. Books on shelves. Neon sign saying "neon." Comfortable old couch and chairs.

✓Top of Empire State Building. Railing. White and blue sky. A pay telescope.

✓Turret of a medieval castle. Stormy night.

THE "WHAT" OR DOMINANT IMAGE

If story or plot is the backbone of a play, the "What," the writer's dominant emotional image, functions as its heart.

The "What" is an image you choose, or that you have allowed to choose you. That image is your source of inspiration. The "What" is the image you hold in mind as you write.

How to find a "What"? One way is to allow an image from a dream to remain in the background of your waking mind. Don't analyze that image, just observe it. (A "What" is not a "theme" arrived at intellectually.)

The "What" image must hold some intrigue or mystery for you. To sustain you as you write, a "What" must imply subtle questions to which you don't have all the answers.

Committing to a "What" commits your work to a chosen emotional territory. If you don't consciously commit to a "What," you may unconsciously choose several "Whats" in succession, unintentionally causing your play to end up all over the map.

Choosing a dominant image, or "What," is a way of choosing the emotional world of your play. Keeping the "What" in mind as you write allows that world to grow and transform in unpredictable ways while remaining cohesive. Don't predetermine how the "What" will be expressed in your writing. Just keep the image in mind as you write. As you write, the "What" is like a secret scent you are inhaling.

In reading a play, the playwright's "What" can often be discovered in its title, as in *Streetcar Named Desire* or *Cat on a Hot Tin Roof*. A literal cat with burning paws is obviously not the subject of *Cat on a Hot Tin Roof*. But, probably without Tennessee Williams' planning it out beforehand, his subtle "What" permeates the personality of several characters as well as the rhythm of the play's language.

➤Make up a list of ten "Whats."

➤Name each "What" in a couple of words. The name should evoke the "What," not generalize it.

➤A "What" also implies its opposite. ("Cutting loose" is at the opposite end of the same emotional territory as "tied up." One implies the other.)

➤The "What" must be in some way active as well as specific. For example, "boredom" is not a good "What," nor is "inferiority complex."

EXAMPLES OF "WHAT"

✓Cutting Loose

✓Red Bird, Purple Sky

✓Touching Base

✓Facing It Out

✓Nut Cracking

✓Silent Scream

✓Lioness in the Neighborhood

THE "WHAT" IN TENNESSEE WILLIAMS

Williams may be America's premiere playwright; he wrote four or five truly fine plays. In part because he is so specific a poet of his home, the American South, Williams' plays are produced and appreciated all over the world. Williams seems to compassionately "hear" and record the rhythms of his idiosyncratic, touching, and often humorous characters without ever patronizing them or turning them into stereotypes.

In Williams' work, there's a sense of unexpectedness — you feel that he doesn't know where his writing will lead him. He starts on a path, then courageously follows it, unafraid to explore the less socially acceptable parts of himself, including his feminine side. (In a mainstream theater in which it was taboo to express overt homosexuality, Williams allowed his own androgyny to surface in some of his characters.)

The atmosphere of Williams' plays seems to draw on the sultry warmth of the South. Deep emotions rise up through his characters as if from underground pools and caverns, surfacing dramatically in lush leaves of language and extravagant blossomings of personality.

Blanche in *Streetcar* is probably the most brilliant and tropical of Williams' characters, a hothouse bloom, sensual, isolated, brightly colored and past her prime.

Williams intends us to experience the truth of our emotions despite the lies which surround us. He sees "mendacity," a favorite word in *Cat on a Hot Tin Roof*, as an underlying disease, the source of personal and societal insanity. He implies that as long as we lie to ourselves, we can't heal or grow. Generalizing a little for the sake of creating an exercise (which will be assigned later), Williams' overall "What" might be called "Mendacity," or "Lying."

ASSIGNMENTS

1. *Overheard Voices*

2. *Who, Where, What*

> ➤Choose one "What" from your list. Write the "What" at the top of a blank page.

> ➤Choose one "Where" from your list. Copy the description of the "Where."

> ➤Choose a "Who" from your list. Copy that character's description.

Imagine the character you chose in the space you chose. You are now responsible for each successive moment of theatrical space and time. In the present tense, write what the character says and does in the space. (What is the character saying or doing now, and now, and now? Nothing can happen on stage "for a while.") Don't write what the audience can't see or hear. Use standard play form. (Character's name comes before the character speaks, indent stage directions, etc.) No character enters or leaves the stage until you are instructed. Don't stop writing until time is up. Keep the "What" in mind.

⊕Writing time: one and a half minutes.

Now choose a second character from the "Who" list. Copy that character's description into the stage directions. The second character enters. Continue writing.

⊕Writing time: six minutes.

Listen carefully to the characters. Observe what is happening rather than forcing something to happen. First character leaves (for reasons you don't need to explain). Second character is alone on stage.

🕐 *Writing time: one minute.*

3. *Suggested Reading*

Death of a Salesman by Arthur Miller.

Workshop Three

PLOT: PLAYWRIGHT AS GUIDE ON THE JOURNEY

OVERHEARD VOICES

Remember, *Overheard Voices* reveals the difference between what we think we hear (which is usually what we expect to hear) and what we actually hear, the unique ways people actually speak. Training the ear in this way increases a playwright's potential for writing exciting, rather than stereotypical, dialogue.

Press your "mental playback button" and write down two or three exchanges of *Overheard Voices*.

⏱ *Writing time: four minutes, plus one more minute if needed.*

Then, read back what you wrote.

READ BACK: *WHO, WHERE, WHAT*

Read back your *Who, Where, What* exercise. Don't worry about how good it is.

Listen attentively to others reading back. Are the rules of the game followed? Do the characters enter and leave according to the instructions?

Has the playwright "listened" to the characters? Do they sound as alive as people in *Overheard Voices*? Can you sense the "What"?

PLOT

A story or plot provides a play with its ongoing linear element, its "horizontal" aspect. It grounds the play in space and time.

During the sixties, a time of experimentation with rule-breaking, people invented "happenings," theater events with no story. The failure of these events to hold interest reaffirmed the need for story. But, although there needs to be some story, the story need not be complex. (Two men waiting for word from God was story enough for Samuel Beckett to write *Waiting for Godot*.)

A play's story can come from many different sources. The ancient Greek playwrights transformed god and hero tales cherished by their community into plays. Shakespeare borrowed the stories for his history plays from Holinshed's *Chronicles*.

Whatever the source of story, a playwright must be personally committed to his or her subject matter. The story you choose for a plot must have deep meaning to you, even if your play is not entirely based on your own experience. The plays of the late nineteenth-century Norwegian playwright Henrik Ibsen and the Russian playwright Anton Chekhov tower above the melodramas that immediately preceded them partly because both these playwrights were, in different ways, passionately involved with the people and historical events of their time and place. A tale told about Ibsen by his great-grandson reveals how even a playwright primarily concerned with justice and social questions writes from a personal place. In a draft of *A Doll House* which he showed his wife, Ibsen did not have Nora leave her oppressive husband at the end of the play. Mrs. Ibsen reportedly reacted by saying, in effect: "Either she goes, or I go."

Arthur Miller also writes about questions of right and wrong, and his questions are not abstract either. In Miller's *Death of a Salesman*, just as in Ibsen's *A Doll House*, moral issues are embodied in characters that moved their author. Chekhov's affair with a young actress probably inspired the character of Nina in *The Sea Gull*. The French playwright Jean Genet's powerful gay erotic fantasies about the murderers, thieves and liars he met in prison inspired his play *Deathwatch*. The audience watching a play may live in a different time and place and lead lives which on the surface are utterly different from those of the playwright, yet we may be personally touched because the playwright was so deeply and specifically involved with the characters and story of his or her play.

Think of a play as a dramatic question, not an answer. Think of yourself as skillfully including the audience in the questions of the play. As you plan the play's journey maintain a confident yet questioning attitude.

Make events as specific as possible. Specifics convey more than generalities. An effective story gives specific details, yet leaves space, questions, around those details for the imagination of the listeners. The philosopher Walter Benjamin gives as example a story about one ancient king captured by another. All the subjects of the captured king are paraded in front of him on their way to be killed. The king remains stony-faced as his army and family pass by. But when an old servant passes by, the king bursts into tears. Why just then? People have been wondering for thousands of years.

PLANNING THE THEATRICAL JOURNEY

Plays are imaginary journeys. Plan a play as you would plan a journey. You don't have to know exactly where you're going, but you do need to know where the path starts and in what general direction it seems to lead. It is useful to have a map of one sort or another. How detailed a map, how elaborately you set up the writing games before you start to write, is up to you. *After* you've written a section — but not *during* writing time — you may decide to revise the shape of your map. Your play may creatively go in directions you had not originally thought about.

Western theater's origin is in the Mystery play, a secret physical and emotional journey planned by priests to lead initiates to drop old ways of seeing the world. A map of the Mystery journey could be a line that starts on middle ground, goes down, then rises up again, ending slightly higher than it started. Initiates descended (like Christ, who "descended into hell") into a dark cave or pit. During their time down there, they were "frightened to death," startled out of their usual habits of thinking. Led back up into light (like Christ who "on the third day ascended into heaven"), they were cleansed with water, invigorated and able to see life in a new way. Like a Mystery play, a contemporary play can be an emotional journey intended to transform vision.

By the time Sophocles wrote Oedipus, theater existed in Greece was much as we know it, with plays which were not just ceremonies only for the privileged as the Mysteries were, but which were presented to the whole community. Instead of priests officiating, playwrights, actors, and musicians provided a vicarious experience to more or less the entire town assembled in one place, a seated audience.

In his *Poetics*, Aristotle, who probably had been initiated into the Eleusinian mysteries, prescribes a few classical rules for playwrights. He states that a play needs a climax to effect an emotional resolution, a catharsis, in the audience.

Aristotle also states that a play's action should take place within a single day and night. Even if that rule is not followed literally, some feeling of unity in a play makes the audience feel safe, cradled by the play's form.

Here are some generally followed rules for contemporary plays:

➤The beginning of a play needs to "hook" the audience.

➤Just before intermission is traditionally a "high" moment ("Make them want to come back for more.")

➤Any act may start slowly but needs a climax before it ends.

➤A play should end on a striking image ("Always leave them laughing.")

Centuries of playwrights have learned that you violate the common sense rules of writing at the risk of losing your audience's interest. Having said this, the theater is a place to vary and break rules. Don't break rules, though, till you've learned them.

For each play, the rules of the game you set up before writing will vary. The novelist Ernest Hemingway said he wrote to find out "what's at the end of my pencil." Openness to adventure as you write may be the basis of creativity, but to write without a plan won't produce work that will hold your own interest long, much less an audience's. To over-plan, on the other hand, leads to a hollow and stereotypical play. Each playwright must find a comfortable middle ground. An ideal plan inspires and supports you as you write, but does not constrict.

The playwright goes on the theatrical journey first, by writing the play. Thus, the playwright knows "where" the audience is at any given moment — high on an emotional peak, crossing a tragic desert, relaxing at a comedic oasis, or left hanging at cliff's edge just before intermission. The playwright is the journey's guide.

A play's shape does not need to be chess-like and logical. Any good play has more than a horizontal movement forward. You might think of your play's journey as a descending spiral (like Dante's *Inferno*), or a shape might be suggested by an archeological or architectural model, or a baseball diamond, or a musical form, or a theory of physics, or a cathedral or a folk dance. To structure a play, use any material that inspires you; use what you know and research what interests you. In *Death of a Salesman*, Arthur Miller skillfully moves the action back and forth in time.

If you want, be outrageous. (For instance, why not a theater of transportation in which the audience is brought from the city into the countryside?) When the impresario Diaghilev was asked by the writer Jean Cocteau what was expected of him, Diaghilev answered, "Surprise me!" Surprise is a virtue in theater, yet the more unique your form, the greater your responsibility to clarity. The audience will welcome the unusual, even the shocking, if they feel grounded and secure in your hands, if you are committed to the shape you have chosen and to your "What," and if you "listen" to your characters.

ASSIGNMENTS

1. *Overheard Voices*

2. Be ready to tell a brief story about an event that happened to you. Choose a story vivid to you but one that holds some mystery.

3. *Who, Where, What — II*

➤ Pick a "What" from your list or create a new one. Write it at the top of a page.

➤ Pick a "Where" from your list or invent a new one. Write a brief description of it.

🕐 *Writing time: one minute.*

➤ Pick two "Whos" from your list or you may invent new ones, following the rule used previously — In creating a character, combine made-up traits with traits of people you know. Whose traits you use remains your secret. Write a brief description of both characters.

🕐 *Writing time: one minute.*

➤ Both characters are in the space. Neither leaves and no one else enters. Let the "What" inspire you. "Listen" to the characters.

🕐 *Writing time: ten minutes.*

➤ Write a brief description of a third character.

🕐 *Writing time: one minute.*

➤Third character enters. The others do not leave. Continue the scene.

🕐 *Writing time: one minute.*

➤One of the two original characters leaves (for reasons not explained). Don't stop to think. Dare to be stupid. Continue the scene.

🕐 *Writing time: five minutes.*

Workshop Four
STORY

ECHOED OVERHEARD VOICES

Echoed Overheard Voices trains the ear while energizing the speaker, giving her or him confidence to read back *Overheard Voices* without hesitation. This exercise requires at least one other person. If you are working alone, get a friend to help.

Write and read back *Overheard Voices*.

➤With everyone present standing (in a circle), each, in turn, speak aloud one short phrase from his or her *Overheard Voices*.

➤Everyone in unison repeats exactly what she or he heard.

➤Then the speaker repeats it, making any adjustments needed in tone, pitch and rhythm to the group's echo.

➤The group echoes again.

➤Do this back and forth three or four times.

READ BACK: *WHO, WHERE, WHAT — II*

Read back your *Who, Where, What — II* exercise.

TELLING A STORY

This exercise is telling aloud a story of something that happened to you. It is a development of the work started in Workshop One. If you are working alone, invite a friend or two to hear you or speak into a tape recorder.

Stand where you can see everyone, with enough space around you to feel free to move. Remember the three moments of preparation. (Center yourself and feel grounded, connect with your listeners by glancing at them, and step forward as you start.)

When you start speaking:

➢Speak in the first person.

➢Speak in the present tense. (The theater is a series of imagined nows.)

➢Be as specific as you can about what you see, hear, taste, smell or touch. Be the spokesperson for your five senses rather than only your ideas.

➢Speak with commitment rather than hesitation.

➢Allow emotion to enter your voice. If you were to cry while speaking, that would be more than okay, as long as you didn't stop speaking.

➤Allow your body to move as you speak.

➤Allow silences to happen.

➤Don't connect thoughts with the word "and." Instead of automatically saying "and" before every new thought or sentence, take a breath. (This is not so simple, but doing it will greatly clarify your story-telling.)

➤Don't start by telling your feelings about the story.

➤Don't offer apologies, judgments, or explanations.

➤Don't maintain any one attitude throughout the story. Tell only what touches you (not what you think you are required to tell).

LISTENING TO STORIES

Listen to others' (or your own tape-recorded) stories with an open, childlike attitude. Allow yourself to be awed, surprised. Avoid negative "objective criticism"; be subjective, positive, and generous in your feedback.

CREATING A SOLO PERFORMANCE PIECE

Telling a Story may serve as the first step toward creating a solo performance piece for yourself. An effective way to create a solo piece is to tape-record yourself telling a story (or stories) and then listen to the recording. Afterward, tell the story into the tape recorder again, making any revisions and additions you wish.

This alternation of speaking and listening to yourself is an "on your feet" (and surprisingly painless) way to "write" and edit a solo performance piece. If you wish, you may at any point transcribe what you've spoken into written form, edit it, and then tell it into the tape recorder again. (You may choose to write other plays this way too.)

When you're ready, invite a friend or two to hear you, and perhaps a potential director. Then, using what feedback you've heard, continue to rework and revise in the same way: recording your work and listening to it. Soon you'll be ready for a larger audience.

ASSIGNMENTS

1. *Overheard Voices*

2. *Hothouse*

"What": Lying.

"Where": Inside the Orchid House of a municipal botanical garden. Evening, winter: icicles visible through the greenhouse glass while inside it is hot, a few orchids brightly blooming.

"Who":

> ✓Henry Sparks, 45, the Orchid House curator. Elegant gardening clothes, nervous, smooth.

> ✓Emma, 25, Raincoat over business suit, boots, attaché case, attractive, looks harried.

> ✓Fred, 19, a part-time worker at the Orchid House, attractive, athletic, t-shirt which says "Orchid."

> ✓Lillian Sparks, 67, Henry's mother. Elegant, carefully dressed, witty, intense, a subtly predatory look.

Look over the characters and scenes, then make a few notes for yourself about their possible conflict. Consider the following questions: Does Henry know Emma before she bursts into the Orchid House? What does Emma really want there? Are Emma and Fred lovers? If so, what are Henry's feelings about this? Are Henry and Fred lovers? What does Fred want from Henry,

Henry from Fred? What does Fred want from Emma? What does Lillian want from her son? How does Lillian control Henry? What does Henry want from his own life?

Don't be satisfied with obvious answers. The characters themselves probably couldn't answer most of these questions unambivalently. Remember the "What" is Lying. Truth is often revealed in layers. The more subtle your insights into the characters and their conflicts, the more subtle your writing. Don't try to know all the answers before you start writing, just know a direction of questioning that intrigues you. The rest you'll learn as you write, by breathing in your image of the "What," and by "listening" to your characters. Let the characters surprise you.

Don't relate to just one character in a scene. As soon as two or more people come together, a unique relational universe is created. Don't predetermine that characters must be "angry," or "friendly," or have any other attitude. Rather, watch and listen to them questioningly in order to "hear," "see," "smell," "touch," and "taste" the nuances of their relationships as those nuances develop. As you write, question the boundaries of relationships; notice how they change. Don't force relationships to change, *allow* them to change.

Scene One: Henry alone in the Orchid House. (This scene, although silent, may require a little research on the specifics of orchid-raising.)

⏱ *Writing time: two minutes.*

Scene Two: Emma bursts into the Orchid House.

🕐*Writing time: five minutes.*

Scene Three: Fred enters. Henry, Emma, and Fred.

🕐*Writing time: two minutes.*

Scene Four: Emma leaves. Henry and Fred alone.

🕐*Writing time: five minutes.*

Scene Five: Lillian arrives, Fred leaves. Henry and Lillian alone.

🕐*Writing time: seven minutes.*

➤Write the following stage direction:

> "Henry drops a potted orchid, breaking the pot. A short silence."

➤Continue writing the scene.

🕐*Writing time: three minutes.*

Scene Six: Henry walks Lillian out. Emma and Fred enter from different parts of the greenhouse.

🕐*Writing time: four minutes.*

Scene Seven: Emma leaves and Henry returns. Henry and Fred alone.

🕐*Writing time: two minutes.*

Scene Eight: Fred leaves. Henry alone. Silent scene. Describe Henry's actions in the Orchid House.

🕐 *Writing time: one minute.*

3. Suggested Reading

Endgame or *Waiting for Godot* by Samuel Beckett.

Workshop Five

THE WORLD OF SAMUEL BECKETT

OVERHEARD VOICES

Dialogue that makes a play exciting, funny, and poignant is not merely spoken information but an expression of the unique vocal rhythms of the characters. To write such dialogue you need first to learn how to hear it in everyday speech.

➤Write and read back *Overheard Voices*.

READ BACK: *HOTHOUSE*

In this, as in any reading, you can ask other people to read aloud with you (if you provide them with legible scripts).

THE WORLD OF SAMUEL BECKETT

We learn from master playwrights by imaginatively exploring their process, allowing their playwriting assumptions to inform ours, to enrich our own imaginative and writing practices.

Innovative playwrights provoke us to see and think in a new way. When we become accustomed to seeing in this new way, we label their work traditional. Why explore Beckett? We more or less still share the world Beckett explores, so his plays may yet shock us out of our usual way of seeing. If we lived in the time of Shakespeare, Ibsen, or Chekhov, we'd probably experience their plays as dramatic changes from our usual way of seeing.

It's unfortunate that Beckett is often considered to be a playwright difficult to understand. In the sixties the Open Theater staged a production of Beckett's *Endgame* for inmates at the prison at Ossining, New York. Most of the prisoners had never seen a play before. Since they had never heard that Beckett's plays were difficult, they were an ideal audience. They roared with laughter at some of Nell and Nag's bawdy lines. They instantly identified with Clove, booed Ham, and cheered when Clove made his final departure. Beckett would have been delighted.

As a playwright, Beckett seems to work by "subtraction," to challenge himself to write within narrow formal parameters in order to express the fierce human desire to live, even in the face of overwhelming loss. In one of his plays only the moving lips of a single character are visible. In another, the actors' bodies are in opaque jars. Beckett seems to be asking how far life can be reduced and still be life.

Beckett does not write abstractly for abstraction's

sake; he's not playing an intellectual game. His work, like that of all playwrights, is grounded in his own experience. He could not have written *Waiting for Godot* or *Endgame* without experiencing the holocaust of World War II. The systematic killing of millions of civilians overwhelmed and changed Beckett's sense of what is basically human.

During the war Beckett was part of the Paris Resistance, secretly fighting the Nazis. On his way to visit the novelist Nathalie Sarraute, Beckett learned that his Resistance partner had just been arrested. Beckett knew that if he went home he too would be arrested, so he asked Sarraute to hide him in her attic. She said, "My father is hiding there." Beckett lived in her attic with Sarraute's father for about a year. Sarraute's father was short and stocky, while Beckett was tall and thin. Years later, when Beckett himself directed *Waiting for Godot* in Berlin, he cast a short stocky man and a tall thin one.

What is the "What" in Beckett's plays? In *Waiting for Godot*, as the title suggests, the "What" has to do with waiting for word from God. In a concentration camp, where people are routinely tortured, killed, and burned, when all that once mattered — social identity, work, home, health, family, and hope of happiness and longevity — has been ripped away, what's left to call human? Breathing. "Breathing" or "pushing on" may be Beckett's "What."

THE COUPLE

The Couple game is inspired by the plays of Samuel Beckett, especially *Happy Days*.

The Couple is an opportunity to focus full attention on "listening" to and "recording" your characters within their world, without having to worry about structure. Imagine that you are listening to and watching your characters on a particular day in their lives. No day is an "average day." Each day has specific events, specific conflicts.

> ➤ Don't have characters generalize about their lives. In writing dialogue, consider that in order to hold audience interest you can afford about one generalization to fifty specifics (if that many). If the present moment is specific and paramount to the characters, then the play will be dramatic to the audience.

> ➤ Characters never discuss the "What." (To discuss the "What" dissipates its force.)

> ➤ As you write, imaginatively "be" or "hear" each character.

This game is best played when the written instructions can be called out by someone before each writing section. If you are playing the game alone, don't read ahead. Let each new instruction come as a surprise.

> ➤ Pick a "What" (one of your own, or one from the list for the *Who, Where, What* game).

> ➤ Write the "What" at the top of your paper.

> ➤ "Who": A couple living together a long time. One of them is seventy-six. The other is eighty-two. Choose characters who in some way are familiar to you, aspects of whose language and world you know. This will make "listening" to them and knowing their conflicts easier and more accurate. Write the gender, first name, and a few specifics about each character.

> ⏲ *Writing time: one minute.*

➤ "Where": Imagine the couple living in a place where there are objects familiar to you. Choose two objects that stand out in your mind. Describe them. Write in the stage directions that these are the only two objects visible on a bare stage.

🕓 *Writing time: thirty seconds.*

Write the following:

OLDER MEMBER OF THE COUPLE [by name]

What time is it?

YOUNGER MEMBER OF THE COUPLE [by name]

I told you I don't know.

Characters may not leave the stage. No others may enter. Continue the scene.

🕓 *Writing time: three minutes.*

Put a period or dash after the last word you've written. Write the following stage directions:

(Lights go out. In the darkness: magnified sound of wood being sawed. Lights come back up. One of the two objects on stage is gone. [Choose which.])

Continue the scene. The characters don't know or mention that the lights went out. They didn't hear the sound. As much or as little time as you wish has elapsed since the last section. The characters remain absorbed in the immediacy of the emotional moment.

🕓 *Writing time: two minutes.*

Put a period or dash after whatever word you've just written. Write the following:

YOUNGER [by name]

What?

OLDER [by name]

Nothing.

Continue the scene.

◕ *Writing time: one minute.*

Put a period or dash after whatever word you've just written. Write the following stage directions:

(Lights go out. In the darkness, magnified sound of a shovel scraping over slate. Lights come back up. The second object [name it] on stage is now gone.)

Continue the scene. The characters don't notice or mention that the lights went out. They do not hear or mention the sound. As much or as little time as you wish has elapsed since the last section.

◕ *Writing time: two minutes.*

Put a period or dash after whatever word you've just written, and write:

OLDER

What was that?

YOUNGER

What?

OLDER

Nothing.

Continue the scene.

☉ *Writing time: one minute.*

Put a dash after whatever word you've just written.
Write the following stage directions:

> (Lights go out. In the darkness, magnified
> sound of a faucet dripping. Lights come
> back up. The older member of the couple is
> encased in a packing case up to the waist,
> facing the audience.)

The characters will not refer to sound, packing
case, or lights going out. As much or as little time
as you wish has elapsed since the last section. Continue the scene.

☉ *Writing time: two minutes.*

Put a period or dash after what you've just written.
Write:

OLDER

What time is it?

YOUNGER

I don't know.

Continue the scene.

☉ *Writing time: one minute.*

Write the following stage directions:

> (Lights go out. In the darkness, loud sound of hammering. When the lights come back up older member of the couple is encased in the packing case up to the neck, and the younger is encased in a packing case up to the waist, also facing the audience. They are too far apart to touch each other.)

Continue the scene. The characters don't refer to sound, lights out, or packing cases. As much or little time has passed since last section as you wish.

⏲ *Writing time: two minutes.*

Put a dash or period after the word you've just written. Write the following stage directions:

> (Lights go out. In the darkness, magnified sound of teeth clacking.)

When the lights come back up, the older member of the couple is totally encased and has lost the power of speech. The younger is encased up to the neck. Continue the scene.

⏲ *Writing time: two minutes.*

Write a comma after the last word you've written. Write that word again. Write it a third time, followed by an ellipsis (three dots . . .).

Write the following stage directions:

> (Lights go out. In the darkness, sound baby crying. Lights come back up. The younger is totally encased now too. There are two packing cases facing the audience. Lights out. The end.)

READING BACK: *THE COUPLE*

Do the characters have distinct voices? Do they speak in specifics? Can you "hear" the emotional music of their speech patterns? Do they feel familiar, in the sense that you can identify with some of their attitudes? Are they unique rather than speaking in stereotypical phrases? Do the characters discuss the "What" or generalize about their lives?

Notice how, if the rules of this game are followed, the characters in their dialogue and actions are focused on the minutia of their daily lives, not ever discussing aging or dying, while, because of the form of the play, the audience is made acutely conscious of time passing and mortality.

ASSIGNMENTS

1. *Overheard Voices*, listening especially to exchanges using idiomatic phrases and slang words.

2. *Doing Right*

   "What": Doing Right

   "Where":

   ✓An urban family kitchen: rudimentary, clean, a hanging lamp, table with chairs, view from window of a fire-escape.

   ✓Men's locker room: a gym.

   ✓Countryside: a peaceful landscape with the vivid colors of fall, front porch in the foreground.

   "Who":

   ✓Ed Jackson, 45, a businessman with barely moderate success, has a haunted look. A careful dresser, he wears a brown suit to work.

   ✓Stacy Jackson, 33, Ed's second wife, works as a receptionist, uses heavy make-up. She has pierced ears with a row of earrings in each ear and wears bright clothes.

   ✓Eddy Jackson, Ed's son, 19, has a quiet deep gaze. He wears a black tee shirt and black jeans.

   ✓Stan Hernandez, 20, Eddy's friend, wears a worn leather jacket. Stan seems always to be moving and talking fast.

✓Richard Jackson, 70, Ed's father, wears a flannel shirt, jeans and a baseball cap.

Scene One: The locker room. Eddy and Stan.

🕓 *Writing time: five minutes.*

Scene Two: The kitchen. Eddy and Stacy.

🕓 *Writing time: three minutes.*

Scene Three: Ed enters the kitchen. Eddy, Stacy and Ed.

🕓 *Writing time: two minutes.*

Scene Four: Eddy leaves the kitchen. Stacy and Ed.

🕓 *Writing time: five minutes.*

Scene Five: Countryside with front porch. Ed and Richard.

🕓 *Writing time: five minutes.*

Scene Six: The kitchen. Ed and Eddy.

🕓 *Writing time: six minutes.*

Look over the characters and scenes. Consider possible conflicts in light of the "What." Who is doing right or wrong, and in whose eyes? What are the layers of doing rights and doing wrong? Without attempting to tell answers, keep refining the questions you are asking as you plot the journey of these scenes. Don't oversimplify. Consider questions such as: How much are we controlled by forces over which we have no control? By whose values do we live? Is it okay to do something illegal for a moral reason? Is ambition compatible with a good life? Is it possible to live up to a parent's hopes without breaking faith with oneself? Can a father ever accept a son?

Choose specific conflicts that interest you. The play's action will interest the audience only when the conflicts you choose are specific and personally interesting to you (rather than merely what you think is appropriate to the characters).

If, before you start writing, and after considering the characters and their conflicts and determining a probable direction for the plot, you wish to change the order of the scenes, add a character or two, or alter the writing times, do so.

Remember: listen to the characters.

3. Suggested Reading

Harold Pinter's *The Dumb Waiter* (a short play) and *The Caretaker.*

As you read, ask yourself: if I were Pinter, what is the "What" that would be moving me to this result? What is happening under the surface in these plays? What is the emotional landscape? What is the "What" in Pinter's work?

Workshop Six
DIALOGUE AND MONOLOGUES

IDIOMATIC EXPRESSIONS AND WORDS

Notice that *Overheard Voices* reflect local life through local idiom.

No one can pinpoint the instant of a word's birth. New words and phrases aren't consciously created by individuals. Idiomatic words and phrases, often highly poetic, are usually born to a specific group. For instance, students may use new words particular to their school, age, town, or group of schools. New words surface when a group needs to communicate a notion in its own (often playful) way. New idiomatic expressions are signals from a collective psyche and sometimes can be used to great effect in plays; they can be revealing and often humorous. Some new words are soon outmoded but some make their way into popular language. Listening carefully to how people talk also makes available to the playwright a contemporary poetic vocabulary.

OVERHEARD VOICES

Read back *Overheard Voices* as usual.

Now "hear" in your mind's ear the same voices as if they were continuing to speak. The trick in fictionally extending *Overheard Voices* is to continue to "hear" the voices in your mind as you heard them in reality, to "hear" *how* they speak, their rhythms and musicality, rather than to start inventing information. Cultivate this ability in order to write compelling dialogue. Write what the voices say.

⏱ *Writing time: three minutes.*

Read back the original *Overheard Voices* followed by the *Extended Voices*. Do the rhythms of the original and extended voices sound the same or did you stop "listening" and strong-arm the characters to convey information?

READ BACK: *DOING RIGHT*

Are the conflicts specific? Interesting? Do the characters have unique voices?

THE "WHAT" IN HAROLD PINTER

What is the "What" in the Pinter plays you read? (Remember the "What" is the gut of the playwright's process, not merely an "issue" or theme.)

Pinter's "What" seems most clear in *The Dumb Waiter*. Pinter's "What" is a kind of fear, the terror that the other person may annihilate you, that if you reveal any vulnerability or show any anger, the other will (figuratively or literally) slit your throat. So how do you behave when you're afraid any show of vulnerability or aggression will invite death? You walk a tightrope of conventionality, you limit yourself to what is socially acceptable in the situation, to what will least alert others to your fear. A mutual terror results in tense non-communication, as displayed by Pinter's characters. This "What," this fear the other might take a razor to your throat, could be labelled *Razor Blades*.

RAZOR BLADES

"What": Write "Razor Blades" at the top of your paper.

"Where": Write the following:

Urban American drugstore. Two A.M. Harsh fluorescent lights.

"Who": Clerk and customer, of the same gender. Name and describe them.

🕐 *Writing time: one minute.*

Story or event: The purchase of razor blades

by the customer. Neither character leaves the stage. No one else enters.

Avoid the trap of creating a victim and a victimizer. There is paranoia in *both* characters. (You may give each a secret reason for fear.) The "What" is never alluded to by the characters.

⏱ *Writing time: maximum six minutes.*

READ BACK: *RAZOR BLADES*

Because of underlying fear, *Razor Blades* dialogue and behavior is limited to what is safe. In this scene what is safe has strictly to do with buying and selling razor blades.

THE POWER OF THE "WHAT"

As you work on *Razor Blades* you may feel irritable or become tense. That is because of the emotional flavor of this particular "What" and the infectious energy of theater. While writing, rehearsing or performing any scene or play, its "What" may exert a powerful spell on everyone involved (including, hopefully, the audience), but when you stop focussing on the scene or play, its emotional flavor dissipates. (British actors refer to "the Scottish play" rather than speak the name of Shakespeare's tragedy, because for centuries mishaps have occurred in rehearsals and performances of *Macbeth*.)

MONOLOGUES

If Pinter's characters are in mortal fear of each other, resulting in conventional talk and behavior, where then do they express feelings? Feelings are released in monologues, all the more forcefully and eloquently for having been repressed, as if much water or air trapped in a closed container were suddenly pushed out through a pinhole.

The character speaking the monologue is passionately articulate, as if alone and speaking to an invisible best friend. From the speaker's point of view, everyone else on stage disappears. In contrast to a dialogue of safe banalities, a Pinter monologue sparkles with poetic specifics.

I LOVE IT

I Love It, a monologue-writing game, is the emotional opposite of *Razor Blades*. *I Love It* is the "What." Let "It" in *I Love It* stand for any activity you love, such as "I love walking through dry leaves," "I love making chocolate fudge," "I love taking photos of old houses," "I love having coffee alone," or "I love jogging at sunset."

➢Choose an "It" that's active (not "I love reading" or "I love watching television," for instance).

➢Don't choose "I love making love." That would short-circuit the game. (An *I Love It* is fueled with passion anyway.)

In this exercise write for your own voice, not a character's, with all the vocabulary and imagery at your command. Write in the present tense. Speak for your senses — for taste, hearing, seeing, smelling and touching: "It sounds, looks, smells, feels, tastes like this." Bring your imagination, like a camera lens, up close to each sensual event.

Sometimes, pushed by the need to be precise in describing a unique sense experience, a writer passionately leaps to describing a sight in terms of smell, a sound in terms of taste or touch, etc. Shakespeare does this magnificently. Poetic language is found by making this kind of leap.

➤In *I Love It* you may instruct as if giving a recipe: Now you do this. Now you do this.

➤Write in specifics. Avoid generalizing superlatives like "great," "special," "fabulous," "fantastic," "wonderful," "incredible," "unbelievable," "amazing," "awesome," and "extraordinary."

➤Don't try to conclude *I Love It* in the allotted time. (You will go back to it later.)

🕐*Writing time: five minutes.*

READ BACK: *I LOVE IT*

Is the *I Love It* written in specifics, does it avoid generalities, is it in the present tense and does it speak for the senses? Does it feel like an experience rather than sound like an analysis?

ASSIGNMENTS

1. *Overheard Voices*

2. You will need two *I Love Its* for the next workshop.

> ➤Complete the *I Love It* you started. Write a new *I Love It*. Set your own writing times. Edit after writing by reading aloud then cutting what you did not enjoy reading.

Workshop Seven
TERROR AND VULNERABILITY

OVERHEARD VOICES

Write, extend, and read back.

READ BACK: *I LOVE IT*

Read aloud both *I Love Its* — the new one, and the one you started earlier.

Is the *I Love It* in the present tense? Is it specific? Does it speak for the senses? Is it an experience rather than an observation?

DRIVING

Driving uses two "What"s alternately: *Razor Blades* and *I Love It*; the "What" will switch back and forth between *Razor Blades* and *I Love It*. Rather than writing the *I Love It* sections now, insert by halves, when instructed, the two *I Love Its* you have already written. Have them ready.

The first "What" is *Razor Blades*. (Each character is secretly terrified that the other will annihilate him or her, so each behaves and speaks in safe conventionalities, neither aggressively nor vulnerably.)

"Where": Front seat of a moving vehicle on a rainy highway at night.

"Who": Passenger and driver, of the same gender. Give them names. The driver has picked up the passenger hitchhiking a while ago. Describe "Where" and "Who."

☽*Writing time: no more than one minute.*

With *Razor Blades* as "What," write in play form what happens and what is said, if anything, as they drive.

☽*Writing time: two minutes.*

Put a dash after whatever word you've just written. Write the following stage direction:

(Passenger turns on the radio. Music: country rock. Driver snaps off radio.)

"What" switches to *I Love It*. Write passenger's name and assign to the passenger the first half of an *I Love It* you wrote.

☽*Writing time : a few seconds to arrange and mark off pages.*

Write the following stage direction:

(The driver begins to cough, a loud dry hacking cough.)

The "What" switches to *Razor Blades.*

🕐 *Writing time: two minutes.*

Put a dash after whatever word you've just written and write the following:

PASSENGER [use name]

What was that?

DRIVER [use name]

Accident.

PASSENGER

Boy.

DRIVER

Yeah.

The "What" switches to *I Love It.* Write the driver's name and assign to the driver the first half of the second *I Love It* you wrote.

🕐 *Writing time: a few seconds to mark pages.*

The "What" switches to *Razor Blades.* Write the following:

PASSENGER

Another one.

DRIVER

Yeah.

PASSENGER

Really raining, huh?

DRIVER

Yeah.

Continue in *Razor Blades*.

🕓 *Writing time: two minutes.*

Put a dash after whatever word you've just written. Write the following stage direction:

(Driver turns on the radio. Music: "Some-where over the Rainbow.")

"What" switches to *I Love It*. Write passenger's name and assign to the passenger the second half of the first *I Love It*.

🕓 *Writing time: a few seconds to mark pages.*

Write the following:

(Driver coughs.)

PASSENGER

Bad cough?

DRIVER

Yeah.

Continue in *Razor Blades*.

🕓 *Writing time: two minutes.*

Put a dash after whatever word you've just written. Write the following:

(The driver turns the wheel violently.)

PASSENGER

Wow, another one.

"What" switches to *I Love It.* Write driver's name and assign to the driver the second half of the second *I Love It.*

🕐 *Writing time: a few seconds to mark pages.*

Write the following:

PASSENGER

Hey!

(Sound of brakes screeching. Vehicle swerves. Lights out. Sound of a loud crash. The end.)

READING BACK: *DRIVING*

Read back a seamless scene, as if the *I Love Its* were written at the same time as the *Razor Blades* sections.

In *Razor Blades*, does each character tread the tightrope of acceptable speech and behavior, hiding terror and vulnerability? Neither character should be more victim than victimizer.

Are the *I Love Its* in the present tense, specific and sensual?

Notice how the poetic highly charged *I Love It* monologues dramatically alternate with the uptight tense *Razor Blades* dialogue, showing the audience, without having to talk about it, the contrast between the characters' fear of each other and their rich inner lives.

If you repeat *Driving* on your own, do not tailor the *I Love Its* to logically fit the characters' vocabulary or interests as expressed in the *Razor Blades* sections. The *I Love It* monologues are written as if in separate compartments and come as a surprising revelation of character to the audience.

In writing any scene, momentarily switching your "What" to *I Love It*, or to *Razor Blades*, can be a useful tool.

ASSIGNMENTS

1. *Overheard Voices*

   Overhear and write down three short exchanges.

2. Invented *Overheard Voices*

   ➤Invent three short exchanges by "listening" to voices in your mind.

   ➤Don't have a different attitude toward *Invented Overheard Voices* than toward *Overheard Voices*. (Continue thinking of yourself as a conduit for voices heard.)

3. *Suggested Reading*

   At least one of the following:

   Eugene Ionesco's *Bald Soprano, The New Tenant,* or *The Chairs*

   Discover the "What" in Ionesco.

THE POINT OF ABSURDITY

OVERHEARD AND INVENTED OVERHEARD VOICES

Read aloud your *Overheard Voices* and *Invented Overheard Voices* in random order.

If you are listening to others, try to guess which *Overheard Voices* are which. (*Invented Voices* are sometimes identifiable because the writer has "forced" characters to tell information, rather than having "listened" to the rhythm of their interchange.)

CREATING WITHOUT POSSESSING

Don't think of *Invented Voices* as more your creation than just plain *Overheard Voices*. When mentally recording we unconsciously select, edit, and transform. (A fact of modern physics is that by the very act of observing a sub-atomic particle, we change either its location or speed.) In his plays, Shakespeare doubtless used phrases overheard in London and Stratford-on-Avon.

Consider every creative act as one of skillfully allowing something to pass through you. (The less attached you feel to what you've created, the freer you are to create more.)

THE "WHAT" IN EUGENE IONESCO

To be entertaining in theater is valuable, but to be merely entertaining quickly wears thin. Ionesco does not wear thin.

Why does Ionesco create crazy situations? What is Ionesco's deep concern? His characters are middle-class, socially conditioned to a fault, and take themselves all too seriously. Their way of thinking adheres slavishly to conventional logic. If it were the acceptable, polite thing to do, they would casually commit murder. They appear to us both funny and pathetic, imprisoned in behavioral and grammatical conventions they never question. Ionesco dramatizes that absurdity. He is a playwright of what critic Martin Esslin termed the "theater of the absurd."

During the course of a play's action, Ionesco subtly exaggerates the characters' hide-bound world, pushing it to its comic extreme. The characters don't adapt and their prison of conventional thinking is revealed. Still, we sense Ionesco has sympathy for his characters and may feel a little like them. Ionesco's "What" might be: Pushing to the Point of Absurdity.

THE POINT OF ABSURDITY

"What": Pushing to the Point of Absurdity

"Who": Three conventional people. Name them. Describe two of them briefly.

Writing time: one and a half minutes.

"Where": An enclosed conventional space. Briefly describe this space.

🕐 *Writing time: one minute.*

The first two characters are in the space.

🕐 *Writing time: six minutes.*

Briefly describe the third character.

🕐 *Writing time: one minute.*

The three characters are in the space. The third character may come and go. Something the third character keeps doing changes the space, makes it more claustrophobic.

🕐 *Writing time: eight minutes.*

READING BACK:
THE POINT OF ABSURDITY

Are the characters ordinary people in a conventional place? Have you "heard" and recorded them speaking, and perhaps exaggerated their verbal rhythms?

Did you push an element of the situation to the extreme? Despite their environment growing increasingly absurd, do the characters implacably retain their conventional behavior and language? Do you have compassion for them, ensnared as they are in society's idea of how to speak and behave (as to some extent we all are)? Did you laugh? (Characters who take themselves dead seriously are funny.)

ASSIGNMENTS

1. *Overheard Voices*

2. Being Respectable

   "What": Being Respectable

   "Where": Any specific "respectable" place, such as someone's dining room, a government office, a library, etc. Describe the "Where."

   ⏲ *Writing time: brief.*

   "Who": describe seven specific characters to whom the following applies:

   Character A always says the opposite of what he or she means.

   Character B invariably agrees with **Character A**.

   Character C will say anything to be loved.

   Character D speaks only in the third person but only of self.

   Character E wishes to reassure everyone that everything is alright.

   Character F is in love with **Character D**, but playing hard to get.

   Character G is playing, well, the role of a human being, but is actually from a planet in a faraway solar system.

   ⏲ *Writing time: no more than a minute for each character.*

Scene One: Characters A, B, and C are on stage.

🕐 *Writing time: three minutes.*

Scene Two: Characters A, B, C, and D are on stage.

🕐 *Writing time: three minutes.*

Scene Three: Characters D, E, and F are on stage.

🕐 *Writing time: three minutes.*

Scene Four: Characters D, E, F, and G are on stage.

🕐 *Writing time: three minutes.*

Scene Five: All characters are on stage.

🕐 *Writing time: five minutes.*

3. Rules

"What": Rules

"Where": Dinner Table. It may be a family event. Choose a conventional place. Describe it briefly.

🕐 *Writing time: thirty seconds.*

"Who": Five people eating a meal together. Write name, age, and brief descriptions of each.

🕐 *Writing time: five minutes.*

Characters are pleasant, polite and appropriate to the situation. They obey unspoken rules against:

✓Describing suffering in detail.

✓Describing dying in detail.

✓Spontaneously expressing love.

✓Using words in highly ungrammatical sequence.

. ✓Crying.

✓Screaming.

✓Addressing people absent or dead.

✓Addressing God.

✓Speaking or behaving in a way not age or gender appropriate.

✓Doing or saying anything that would be unacceptable on a soap opera.

⊕ *Writing time: four minutes.*

First character announces, "I shall now break the rule against——." That character proceeds to break that rule (chosen by you from the rules above), during which the other characters are silent (like characters in *Razor Blades* during an *I Love It*).

⊕ *Writing time: two minutes.*

All continue to obey the rules as if nothing had happened. They do not comment on what happened.

⊕ *Writing time: two minutes.*

A second character announces, "I shall now break the rule against———." That character breaks that rule.

🕐 *Writing time: two minutes.*

All continue to obey the rules as if nothing had happened. They don't comment on what happened.

🕐 *Writing time: two minutes.*

A third character announces, "I shall now break the rule against———." That character proceeds to break that rule.

🕐 *Writing time: two minutes.*

All continue to obey the rules as if nothing had happened. They don't comment on what happened.

🕐 *Writing time: one minute.*

Fourth character announces, "I shall now break the rule against———." That character proceeds to break that rule.

🕐 *Writing time: four minutes.*

All continue to obey the rules as if nothing had happened. They do not comment on what happened.

🕐 *Writing time: three minutes.*

The fifth character announces, "I shall now break the rule against screaming." Write that the character breaks that rule loudly for a long time, then lights out.

4. *Suggested Reading*

Bertolt Brecht's short play *The Exception and the Rule*. If you can find a recording, listen to the Brecht/Weill musical, *The Threepenny Opera*, or read the text. Discover the "What" in Brecht.

THE ALIENATION EFFECT: WATCH HOW PEOPLE USE PEOPLE

ROUND ROBIN OVERHEARD VOICES

Begin with *Overheard Voices*.

🕐*Writing time: three minutes.*

Round Robin Overheard Voices can be played only in a group. Fold your paper so that just the final couple of lines of your last *Overheard Voices* are visible. Pass that paper to a writer near you.

Read to yourself the lines you have received.

Invent *Overheard Voices* for the next lines of these characters. Focus on continuing the rhythm of the characters' voices rather than adding information.

🕐*Writing time: one and a half minutes.*

Fold your paper so only the last couple of lines you wrote are visible. Pass the paper to a person who has not already worked on those *Overheard Voices.* Read to yourself the lines you have received.

Continue the same steps until everyone has added to each paper and you receive back your own.

Read to yourself only the last couple of lines, remembering the rhythm and musicality of your original characters. Write the next lines of these characters.

⏱ *Writing time: one and a half minutes.*

Read aloud everything on the paper you are holding, as you would any *Overheard Voices.*

While listening, hear if the writers connected to the unique voices of the characters.

READ ALOUD:
BEING RESPECTABLE AND *RULES*

This should be fun.

THE "WHAT" IN BERTOLT BRECHT

What do Brecht's characters state they are doing to each other? There is a lyric in *The Threepenny Opera*: "What keeps a man alive? He lives on others." Brecht's "What" might be called Living On Others or Watch How People Use People.

Brecht is (to borrow the name of his play) an exception to the rule. This is true in two ways. His "What" is always political and his characters repeatedly state the "What."

Brecht's "What" is emphasized by the famous Brechtian acting style, the "alienation effect," in which the actor while performing seems to be pointing to his or her character and saying, "Look, look, what is happening to my character now."

Brecht, as any playwright, wants his audience to identify with the characters, but he also wants his audience to constantly consider the wider political implications of what is happening. Brecht's use of a deliberately stated "What" has influenced many modern plays and musical plays.

Brecht poses political questions in a skillful, theatrical way. He nudges us to think but doesn't provide answers. If he did, we would be less interested in his questions. If an audience isn't emotionally involved in a play's action, or entertained, it won't be open to the playwright's ideas. Playwrights can awaken consciousness only if their plays are successful dramatically and if they don't try to preach.

WATCH HOW PEOPLE USE PEOPLE

"What": Watch How People Use People

"Where": A town like but not identical to your town. Give the fictional town a name and create a list of interior and exterior "Wheres," naming them playfully. The following examples are from lists created at the University of Colorado, Boulder. Your lists will, of course, be different.

✓ Dean's office, Moulderado University

✓ Mayor's office

✓ Rocky Horror Beauty Place

✓ University Library, the basement

✓ Rowboat's dorm room

✓ Fanny Mymy's dressing room

✓ Dr. Mel Swoonbait's office

✓ The Crusty living room

✓ Hubie's Healthy Nuts, eatery

✓ Dizzy's Discoria

✓ Lydown Lagoon, massage parlor

"Who": Create a list of who lives in the town. Because the "What" is so explicit, Brechtian characters have a touch of caricature. Examples:

✓Rowboat Paramount, undergraduate, 20

✓Maria Winner, undergraduate, 19

✓Fanny Mymy\Andy Jones, drag artist and accountant, 38

✓"Nose," alcoholic, panhandler, 35

✓Dr. Mel Swoonbait, dentist, 32

✓Laura Jenesaisquoi, Swoonbait's nurse, 37

✓Frank Dullknife, graduate student in English, 24

✓Cora Upt, Mayor of Moulderado, 40

✓I. M. Crusty, Trustee, Moulderado U., 80

✓Jessica Crusty, undergraduate, granddaughter of I. M.

✓Ray C. Pomposo, Philosophy Professor, 58

✓Lips Irvis, President, Moulderado U., 48

WRITING SONGS

A play has "horizontal" and "vertical" dimensions. The "horizontal" has to do with duration, a ribbon of events following each other in time. The "vertical" has to do with deepening and heightening emotions in the present moment. A song, like an *I*

Love It, usually performs a "vertical" function. (Some songs, of course, also advance the action.)

Playing with music and songs in a play can be great fun and has a long tradition. Music and dance have been part of theater since the ancient Greeks. Songs, like poetry, likely existed before the written word. From *Overheard Voices,* it's a short, easy jump to spoken words with music.

If you've never written a song, just plunge in and do it in a playful way. One way is to repeat a phrase of *Overheard Voices* over and over until the rhythmic repetition suggests a simple tune, then add to that phrase and tune. Or, for purposes of this exercise only, take an existing tune you like and write your own words to it. Or you may choose to write a full-fledged song lyric and to ask a composer friend to compose music for it.

A song lyric is rarely as concentrated as a poem. A lyric is closer to everyday speech. A lyric needs "space" between the words to make room for the music. Broadway songwriter Stephen Sondheim said, "If you wrote 'Oh, what a beautiful morning, oh what a beautiful day, I've got a wonderful feeling, everything's going my way,' it would be a disappointing poem. As a lyric, of course, it's ideal." A Brecht lyric is more condensed but still close to everyday speech, as in *The Threepenny Opera*: "Let's all go barmee. Let's join the army, see the world we've never seen. And if the population should treat us with indignation, we'll chop them to bits because we like our hamburgers raw."

Although the names of characters and places in this exercise have an element of caricature, don't patronize your potential audience by writing these scenes in too simple-minded a way. A character who is a user in one scene may in the next be the victim in a different way. "Listen" to your characters as you do in *Overheard Voices*, especially for local idiomatic expressions.

"What": Watch How People Use People. Keep this "What" not only in your mind but also in the audience's.

"Wheres" and "Whos" are from your lists.

As introduction, a character speaks to the audience about the "What" in relation to other characters in the play.

🕐 *Writing time: three minutes.*

A scene which starts the action. Have a specific conflict in mind. Describe "Where" and "Who." Write a placard to inform the audience of "Where" and perhaps "What" is happening. Write the scene.

🕐 *Writing time: six minutes*

Song by character(s) on local specific subject related to the "What."

🕐 *Writing time: six minutes or more.*

Second scene, using no more than one of the characters from the first scene. Describe "Where" and "Who." Write a placard for the audience. Write the scene.

🕐 *Writing time: six minutes.*

A character speaks to the audience on a local specific subject related to the "What."

🕐 *Writing time: three minutes.*

If you are inspired to do so, continue in the same vein with as many scenes and songs as you like.

READ BACK:
WATCH HOW PEOPLE USE PEOPLE

Remember that you may ask other people to join you in reading aloud.

In listening, in this exceptional case, is the "What" explicit throughout? Is the "What" expressed humorously and intelligently? Can you hear the musicality in each character's voice? Do the different kinds of scenes follow each other interestingly? Do you like the song(s)?

ASSIGNMENTS

1. *Overheard Voices*

2. Before sleep, tell yourself to remember a dream when you awake. Keep a notebook or tape recorder by the bed. Record your dream immediately on awakening or you may forget it. To help remember, you might want to reassume the body shape in which you awoke by finding the warm spots in the bed.

3. *Suggested Reading*

Read the first chapter of Antonin Artaud's *The Theater and Its Double* thoroughly. Then dip into the book and read whatever interests you.

Workshop Ten

DREAMS AND CEREMONY

VERHEARD VOICES

Overheard Voices as usual.

HE THEATER AND ITS DOUBLE

Not only can anything happen in theater, but it is good that extreme events should occur on stage; it is theater's job to be dramatic.

In life it's bad to kill one parent and sleep with another. But when Oedipus does it on stage, it's good. Why? Because with no one really harmed, a powerful emotional journey brings to consciousness a previously denied impulse. Someone in the ancient Greek audience of *Oedipus Rex* may have dramatically realized: "Ah hah, yes, I too want to kill my father and sleep with my mother." Theater can be exorcism. If a play is moving on a deep level, first the playwright, then the performers, and ultimately the audience take a personally significant emotional journey. As in psychotherapy, emotionally admitting up to impulses eventually leads to healing. Images in live theater can profoundly affect individuals and, ultimately, society, performing a subtle healing that has nothing to do with preaching. Granted, only the best of theater does this. But why not aim for the best?

Theater, like dreaming, is a safe context within which to experience cruel (in the Artaudian sense) dramatic events and the wobbling of our usual straight-line thinking. Having this experience theatrically, we become more open to hearing life's subtle emotional messages.

A play's journey starts when the playwright courageously plumbs her or his own dreaming depths for specific images that ask questions (the "What"). If the images come from a place deep enough, and if the playwright and the performers give them voice with commitment and skill (including humor), the images will communicate personally to audiences.

Does deep communication occur with every play? Alas, no. Artaud passionately insists that theater be more than it usually is. He wants theater reunited with its shamanistic roots. Artaud inspires some of the best practitioners of theater and is the standard bearer of theater's crazy wisdom.

Without looking at Artaud's book now (or at the next paragraphs in this *Workbook*), tell the story Artaud tells in the first chapter of *Theater and Its Double*. Recall precisely what happened, event by event in order, as if you were a detective looking for clues to the nature of communication.

Start with "Where." The events happen on the island of Sardinia. (As in Shakespeare's *Tempest*, a story of events on an island may also be the story of events in an isolated mind.)

What about "Who?" To whom does the main event happen? To the Viceroy, who rules Sardinia with nearly absolute power.

What happens to him? The Viceroy dreams that he suffers from the plague. He doesn't merely dream about the plague, he experiences the plague: huge boils in his armpits and groin, festering wounds, excruciating pain, and fear of imminent death. Then the Viceroy awakens.

What happens next? A ship sailing toward Sardinia signals for help. Contradicting all laws of hospitality, the Viceroy forbids the ship to land. The ship sails on to Marseilles, where, after its arrival, there is a virulent outbreak of the plague.

The telling question is *What is the nature of the deep communication* between ship and Viceroy? Vibes? Spirit? Science has no word for it and although artists may feel it, we can't adequately name it either. However, in the theater what we can do is create conditions that lead to that kind of communication.

TELLING A DREAM

Tell a dream to the group, to a friend, or even to a friendly tape recorder. (You'll learn more if you tell the dream than if you read it aloud.)

Follow the same rules as in *Telling a Story:*

➤Take a moment to center yourself.

➤Look at your listeners, then step forward as you start.

➤Speak in the present tense.

➤Be specific. Don't offer explanations or your overall feeling about the dream. Don't maintain allegiance to any single emotion. (Even a nightmare may have funny moments.) Allow the dream to be different in different moments and respect its unique world.

➤Allow silences. Breathe.

🕑 *Telling time: no more than five minutes.*

LISTENING TO A DREAM

Senoi natives encourage children to tell their dreams every morning and to bring back from dreams something creatively useful, such as a melody or a new weave for a basket. As you listen to the dream, imagine it as a landscape through which the dreamer leads you. What moved you? (Don't try to analyze the dream.)

How can you use this dream artistically? Does the dream contain a "What"? Is there a useful "Who" or "Where" in the dream? Is the dream material for a play?

WHAT MATERIAL IS MOST APPROPRIATE TO THEATER?

Theater doesn't easily accommodate as broad a canvas as, say, an epic novel, or plumb the depths of a single feeling as does a poem. Some dreams, stories, or ideas are better expressed in other art forms. Video can transport you instantly to any place in the global village, film directs your eye to specific visual images. What distinguishes theater from other art forms is the physical presence of actors and audience together in a space. The more imaginatively a playwright exploits this distinction, the more dramatic an event results.

CEREMONY

A ceremony is a dramatic event. Theater started with ceremonies. Ancient priests were, in effect, playwright-actors performing rites of emotional transformation with and for their community.

Planning and celebrating a ceremony is one imaginative way to function as a playwright. Different ceremonies, of course, have different intents, feelings, and tones and demand, therefore, different approaches. As in writing, the logical mind (the left brain) plans or structures the rules of the game, then, secure within those rules, the creative mind (the right brain) executes the ceremony. Success depends on how clear and imaginative the plan is, and how generously the plan is executed. To create a ceremony, research its traditional intent (if any), then plan each step, carefully adapting tradition to the needs of the present. Finally, invite others and perform it.

An example: a tea ceremony. In old Japan the creative link between calligraphy, flower arranging, pottery, and architecture is "tea," the tea ceremony, also sometimes called "the way of tea." An open but attentive attitude in preparing and offering tea is key. The caring performance of simple actions engenders a balanced state of mind. A tea ceremony is performed to quiet the mind in the midst of chaos, to honor someone dead or alive, to make peace, or for any other positive purpose.

In planning a tea ceremony, research its guiding principles and intent. How do you maintain tea's intent while adapting the ceremony to your world? How do you offer guests a tranquil, theatrical time? Do you want to dedicate the ceremony to someone or commemorate an event? If the ceremony is too formal and unfamiliar, guests will feel distanced. If it's too informal, it won't offer a mindful experience. Plan each step, considering how environment, speech, and action will affect experience. How do you invite the guests? How do you create a clean, simple, beautiful space as a "tea house?" Plan the path by which the guests will approach the "tea house." Decide how to greet the guests. Will guests be asked to remove their shoes? Where and how long will they stop to compose themselves before entering the "tea house?" How do you respectfully indicate where guests may sit, and set a mindful tone? Will there be a flower in the tea house? A work of art? Where do you place these? What will be said in greeting? When? How do you make guests comfortable in relative silence? What do you serve as "tea?" (Actual tea requires heating and brewing. Perhaps juice would do. If so, what kind of juice?) What cups or glasses should you use? (What aesthetic and ecological statements are you making by your choices?) What "teapot" or pitcher should you use? What sweet do you have? How and when do you present it? What napkins do you use? What will mark the end of the event? Remember, what matters most is the quality of attention given to planning and performing the ceremony.

ASSIGNMENTS

1. Intimate *Overheard Voices* (a more advanced form of *Overheard Voices*).

> ➤Record brief exchanges between people who know each other well. Listen for those anywhere, in private as well as public spaces. Listen for rhythm and musicality, not merely content.

2. Write a description of a home (house or apartment) you know intimately (but don't describe anyone living in the home).

In your description include answers to the following questions:

✓When was the building built?

✓What state and town is it in?

✓What's the placement of the home in relation to other buildings, roads, bodies of water, mountains, and trees?

✓What's the color and character of the building?

✓What's the dominant smell in the home?

Describe three or four of the home's living spaces. Pick interesting spaces in which people can be together: living room, kitchen, a bedroom, attic, garage, back yard, or front porch. Describe each space after imagining yourself in it. (But don't describe how to get from one space to another.) How big is each space? How does it feel? What are the light sources? What are the striking objects or furniture? What is unexpected in them?

3. *Suggested Reading*

Read Anton Chekhov's *The Cherry Orchard* and *The Sea Gull* in *Chekhov, The Major Plays*, Applause Books, 1995. As you read, ask yourself what is the "What?"

Workshop Eleven
BREAKING GROUND

NTIMATE OVERHEARD VOICES

The reason this is a more advanced *Overheard Voices* exercise is because people who know each other well are more difficult to record accurately. The listener tends to be stirred up by what he or she hears, and may react by unconsciously imposing preconceptions and recording intimate exchanges more stereotypically than they were spoken. Therefore *Intimate Overheard Voices* requires even more careful attention to rhythm, pitch, tone, pauses, and musicality.

Exchanges between intimates are rarely about intimacy. People who know each other well often use few words. Theirs may be a brief ritual duet serving to reaffirm feelings. How something is said, and what is not said, is important. An exchange about a mundane matter may be full of feeling. People may talk about a broken refrigerator while their tone, rhythm, and pitch may reveal lust, love, contempt, or fury. The emotional nail is rarely hit verbally on the head.

➤Write and read back *Intimate Overheard Voices*.

THE "WHAT" IN CHEKHOV

What is Chekhov writing about in *The Cherry Or-chard*? What inspires him? Put yourself in Chekhov's heart and mind. What would move you to write as he wrote? "Depression" is surely not Chekhov's "What." His characters may be sad but they are also joyous. They are sad and funny at the same time. They make us laugh through tears.

"What" is Chekhov about? Philosophizing? Vain hoping? Perhaps, but as "Whats" these are too abstract to inspire. Chekhov was a doctor and a careful and compassionate observer of people. His characters are fun to gossip about. Its fun to discuss what Masha in *The Sea Gull* says, how she says it, why she drinks, and why she wears black. Chekhov's characters are like a family we know well. Masha appears under various names in several different plays (Varya in *The Cherry Orchard*, Masha in *Three Sisters* and *The Sea Gull*, Sonya in *Uncle Vanya*). Why? Perhaps because Chekhov felt close to his sister Maria, and probably drew on his feelings about her to create these moving, complex, funny characters.

As always, look for the "What" in the title. The Cherry Orchard is the name of the house and land. The Cherry Orchard is home. Chekhov's "What" is Home. Home implies its opposite, homelessness; Home implies state of mind, mood of country, philosophy, social class, habits of seeing, and, above all, the family (however extended and disjointed) who lives at home.

We usually feel at home in our present way of thinking. However uncomfortable our thinking habits may be, they are familiar. But in actuality "home," the world, and how we see it, is constantly changing, and dealing with change is painful.

What are some of the characters' feelings about home? Madame Ranevskaya, owner of the Cherry Orchard, adores her home, but from a distance. She's sentimental about the Cherry Orchard but lives in Paris. Her brother, Gaev, is dependent on home, a baby in its maternal embrace. For Varya, home is a place in which to be a caretaker, a place in which she feels secondary. When Varya has a chance to change her status, she cannot. Trofimof, the revolutionary, feels at home only in his idea of the future. Irina, the youngest, is the most hopeful character; when her home changes, she starts to change too. Lopakhin loves home so much he destroys it, takes an axe to it. Firs, the old retainer, is the Cherry Orchard — almost literally. He's inseparable from the house. When axes cut into the trees, it's as if Firs' old bones themselves are axed. When the house dies, Firs dies.

Did Chekhov plan his plays by organizing social, historical, and psychological themes beforehand and assigning them to characters? Probably not. Inspired by a personal image of a loved and threatened home (the "What" and the plot), he chose "Wheres" and "Whos" partly familiar to him, "listened" to his characters and their conflicts, and alternated two-person and group scenes with monologues, like a composer. A master practitioner of playwriting, all he believed in and felt was spontaneously expressed through the right character in the right place at the right moment in the play.

Read the stage directions at the top of the second act: "A meadow, an old abandoned chapel falling over. Next to it a well, some large stones which were probably once tombstones, and an old bench. We see the road which leads to Gayev's house. To one side are several dark poplar trees, and there starts the cherry orchard. Further there is a row of telegraph poles. In the farthest distance, one can guess the outline of a large town, visible only on very clear days. The sun will soon set." Good symbols radiate meaning without representing something other than themselves. Tombstones imply the past, and are useful for sitting. The road comes from the house and goes toward the faraway city. It implies an encroaching industrial future, but it's also just the road.

CHEKHOV AND SOAP OPERA

What's the difference between Chekhov and soap opera? Soap opera uses "Who," "Where," and "What" in ways similar to Chekhov, yet Chekhov hits deep chords while soap opera does not. The intention is different. Soap opera is a commercial enterprise, creating an audience for advertising, while Chekhov intends to plumb the mysterious depths of the human heart. The difference is one of quality. Quality can be felt but not adequately described. In part it results from the playwright's intention and depth of attention, the playwright's ability to "listen."

The word "pause" repeatedly occurs in Chekhov's stage directions. Chekhov is famous for his pauses. There's a moving moment in Act II of *The Cherry Orchard:* "Everyone sits silent, musing. It is quiet. Firs mutters softly to himself. The sound of a rope breaking is heard from far off, coming as if from the sky. Gradually the sound fades, leaving traces of sadness." In the quiet is the quality of listening. The characters listen, and the audience listens. For that subtle event to happen successfully, the playwright had to listen.

"Listen" to characters even when they're not speaking. Characters don't need to be constantly talking. Meaning can make itself felt in silence. Don't rush characters because you're anxious about running short of things for them to say. If, as you write, you feel yourself rushing, becoming merely mental, pushing your characters, then slow down and refocus on your "What." "Listen" not only to the music of your characters' voices, but for the tone of "where they're at." If you respect and listen to your characters, so will the audience.

HOMES DESCRIBED

If you are working alone, use your description of a home for the exercises that follow. If you are working with a group, tell your description of a home without telling your relationship to the home or who lives there. Say: "A house in Santa Monica, California," or "A farmhouse in Lawrence, Kansas," or "An apartment in Brooklyn, New York." Tell approximately when the building was built, the look of it, its relationship to other buildings, roads, trees, hills, or bodies of water. What is the dominant smell inside the home? Without taking listeners on an imaginary walk from one space to another, describe specific "Wheres" inside or outside the home. How does each "Where" feel? What's the dominant color? Is the space welcoming or cold, cared-for or run-down? What are the important objects? (Don't list *all* objects.) Is there anything unexpected? Everyone take notes on all the homes. Vote on one for the group to work on now. (Keep your description of your own home. It will be useful later.)

PEOPLING A HOME

If you are working alone, use your description of a home to do the following work. When inventing "Who," use some traits of people you know, and mix them with other traits, rather than use the exact people who live or lived in the home you described.

➤If you are working in a group, together invent "Who" lives in the home the group voted to work on. (The person whose home was chosen should provide no actual information regarding "Who.")

➤Give a name to the person(s) who owns or pays rent on the home.

➤Give that character or characters an apparent age and important characteristics (as when the class created "Whos").

➤With whom, if anyone, does this person live? Who are the children, parents, lover(s), spouse, roommates, neighbors, ex-lovers, ex-spouses, stepparents, friends, or anyone else who might turn up in the home? When new characters are created, ask who is important to them, thereby creating a network of characters, all related in one way or another to the home. Give each character a name, age, and important traits. Don't create stereotypes. No character exists merely in relation to another. Find character traits that are loveable, and others that are not. Draw on people you know but add other characteristics to them. Create more characters than you'll use (as for *Who, Where, What*). Include a broad age range of characters.

ASSIGNMENTS

1. *Intimate Overheard Voices*

2. Write a history of the characters living in the home you chose. (This is for your own use, to deepen your sense of the characters and their history.)

3. *Home — I*

> Writing scenes which deal with intimate emotions brings up one's own defenses, so be on guard — don't allow anxiety to drive you toward stereotypical writing. Write from a questioning attitude.
>
> Even if you violate the writing rules (for instance, if you write for a longer period of time), the presence of the rules still provides a secure cradle for creativity. Logical mind sets up the rules so creative mind can play within them.
>
> **Scene One**: Choose and briefly describe a specific "Where," in the home. Whether a scene takes place indoors or outdoors, in what season and at what time of day, sets an emotional climate, so include a "When," possibly from one of the following times:
>
> ✓ Labor Day this year, 4:00 P.M.
>
> ✓ Thanksgiving, 11:00 A.M.
>
> ✓ December 22nd, midnight
>
> ✓ June 21st next year, 9:00 P.M.
>
> ⊗ *Writing time: no more than two minutes.*

Choosing from your list, briefly describe two
"Whos."

⏱ *Writing time: two minutes.*

With the two "Whos" you chose on stage,
keeping a personal image of the "What,"
Home, in mind, start the scene.

⏱ *Writing time: six minutes.*

Write into the stage directions that one
character leaves. Continue with the other
character on stage.

⏱ *Writing time: one minute.*

Choosing from your list, briefly describe a
third character.

⏱ *Writing time: one minute.*

Write that the third character enters. Then
continue the scene with the two characters
on stage.

⏱ *Writing time: six minutes.*

Scene Two: Choose and briefly describe another "Where" and "When" from your list.

⏱ *Writing time: one minute.*

From your list, choose and briefly describe
two characters you did not use in the previous scene.

With the two characters on stage, always
keeping the "What" in mind, start the new
scene.

⏱ *Writing time: four minutes.*

One of the characters from the first scene enters. Continue, with the three characters on stage.

⏱ *Writing time: six minutes.*

If you want to write a third (or more) scene(s), set them up as you did the first two. From the list of possible "Wheres" and "Whens," set the stage. Choose from the list who will be there at the start. Describe briefly any characters not seen before. Decide who will leave when and who will enter when. Set up approximate writing times.

4. *Suggested Reading*

Three Sisters and/or *Uncle Vanya* by Anton Chekhov (in *Chekhov, The Major Plays*)

Workshop Twelve

CONTINUING ON YOUR OWN

EXTENDING INTIMATE OVERHEARD VOICES

Being practiced at *Intimate Overheard Voices* facilitates writing emotional exchanges without imposing preconceptions on them.

After reading back, extend your *Intimate Overheard Voices*, or, instead, write one or two new short exchanges for the same speakers.

🕐 *Writing time: no more than one and a half minutes.*

Read back.

In listening to *Extended Voices*, can you recognize the rhythms and tones of the original voices?

READ BACK: *HOME – I*

Are characters as unforced as voices in *Overheard Voices*?

A combination of vivid specifics and interesting gaps makes a "Who" or "Where" stimulating to write.

EDITING

Some playwrights edit and rewrite greatly, some less. However much or little you choose to edit, don't try to write and edit at the same time. Criticizing and creating simultaneously leads to paralysis. When you've finished writing (a creative right-brain process), *then* you can edit (a logical left-brain process), after which, if you like, you can rewrite or write more. In playwriting, logical brain and intuitive brain are used in turn, not simultaneously.

What do you do about critical voices you may hear in your mind as you write? ("This is no good. You're wasting your time. You'll never be a great playwright, not you.") Most of us have private inner critics programmed to carp and nag. It is hopeless to try to suffocate them. It is possible not to heed them. Allow them to make noise while you carry on with your work. It is comforting to note that demonic judges in the mind are likely to be most present when you are being most daringly creative. So, don't take them seriously, just let them scream their insults as you pay attention to your playwriting.

A good way to edit is to read aloud what you've written (whether anyone is present to hear you or not, perhaps into a tape recorder). Notice when, as a performer, you enjoy reading, and notice when you want to rush ahead to more "juicy" parts. The parts you don't enjoy reading are likely material for cutting.

Often the first few lines of a speech, or the first few pages of a scene, while they may have been a necessary exploration for you, are not dramatic enough to offer the audience. Edit so that a scene starts at the point where the characters seem to jump to life.

Cut within speeches by only retaining lines which are fun to speak, specific in imagery, and have the most rhythm.

It helps the pace of a play to edit out unnecessary generalizations, stereotypical polite greetings (most thank yous, hellos, and goodbyes), and lines that hold only explanatory information (traditionally called "feather dusters" because they are spoken in the first scene by a maid dusting the drawing room). Always assume an intelligent, sensitive audience. Assume an audience of friends. It would be patronizing to give friends too much information that they can fill in for themselves.

REWRITING

If you sense a whole scene doesn't "work," write it again, either using the same "Who," "Where," and "What," or changing any of these before you start to write. Changing "Who," "Where," and "What" before rewriting is like reprogramming computer software before using it again.

When rewriting you will know your characters better, so you can "listen" to them better. Don't refer to the first draft while rewriting, . Most of what you like, you'll write again spontaneously. If you want to retrieve something written in the first draft, do so later. Remember that writing and editing are done separately, not simultaneously.

COMPOSING SCENE ORDER: THE BREATHING OF A PLAY

Notice in Chekhov's plays the musical way one scene follows another, as if the play breathes in and out with succeeding scenes alternating in tension and relaxation. A play expands and contracts, breathes, throughout its playing time. A tense moment is followed by release. Moments "breathe" in and out within a scene, scenes breathe within an act, and acts within a play. Tension and release give a play life and encourage the audience to emotionally breathe with the play.

The audience needs moments to absorb, to cry, and to laugh. If, for instance, a play proceeds at a relentlessly high pitch and has no quiet or comedic moments, eventually the audience, emotionally exhausted, will become frustrated and bored. If, on the other hand, a play is only froth with no underlying feeling, the audience will also eventually become frustrated and bored.

One way to arrange the order of scenes in a play is to think of yourself as arranging a sequence of musical pieces for a chamber concert (in which a duet may be followed by a trio, perhaps followed by a solo, etc.). In sequencing scenes and emotional moments, consider: What experience do I want the audience to have *now*, at this moment? And *now*, at this moment?

In structuring the order of scenes, it is useful to consider starting a new scene each time the number of characters on stage changes. (This is the traditional way of numbering scenes in French plays.)

ASSIGNMENTS

1. *Overheard Voices*

2. *Home — II*

> If you are working alone, pick another home you know and describe it as you did the first, including a few "Wheres" within it. If you're working with a group and used for *Home — I* a home that wasn't yours, for *Home — II* use the home you originally described.
>
> ⏲ *Writing time: about fifteen minutes.*

> People this home as for *Home — I.* Don't use actual people you know but mix their traits with other traits. Start with "Who" owns or pays rent on this home. Remember that each related character is the center of her or his own world. Develop a list of at least ten "Whos" from which to draw.
>
> ⏲ *Writing time: about one minute per character.*

> Write (for yourself rather than for the script) a biographical history of your network of "Whos," going as far back in time as you feel is significant.
>
> ⏲ *Writing time: about twenty minutes.*

> Make a list of a few dates and times for scenes you might write.
>
> ⏲ *Writing time: no more than a minute.*

Write the "What" (either *Home* or your personal image of the home you described) at the top of your first page. Choose the first date/time and a "Where" from your list. Describe the "Where" briefly in the stage directions.

⏱ *Writing time: one and a half minutes.*

Pick two characters from your list. Describe them briefly on stage in the "Where" you chose.

⏱ *Writing time: one minute.*

Keeping the "What" in mind, start scene one, the two characters remaining on stage. (Without stopping writing, "listen" to the characters and their conflicts. Don't impatiently force them into doing or saying anything. If *later*, on rereading, you find the beginning slow, you are free to cut it.)

⏱ *Writing time: six minutes.*

A third "Who" enters. Describe that character.

⏱ *Writing time: one minute.*

Continue writing with the three characters on stage.

⏱ *Writing time: five minutes.*

One of the first two characters leaves. Continue writing with the two characters remaining on stage.

⏱ *Writing time: seven minutes.*

One character leaves. Switch "What" to *I Love It*. Follow the rules for *I Love It*. (Write for your own most articulate voice. Don't bend the monologue to fit the character or situation.)

☺ *Writing time: two minutes.*

Write that the lights slowly fade out.

3. Games in this *Workbook* lead to different forms of play. By combining *Workbook* games with those you invent yourself, you can create your own forms. Collect any writing you've done while working with this *Workbook* that you want to work on further.

4. Consider if there is any idea for a play (a personal experience, a political happening, a story, a dream) you might want to write about.

Workshop Thirteen
MOVING TOWARD PRODUCTION

OVERHEARD VOICES

Read back *Overheard Voices* as usual.

Even after you have stopped working with this *Workbook*, remaining alert to music and rhythm in human speech will keep the characters in your plays alive and unique.

READING ALOUD *HOME – II* AND OTHER RECENT WORK

Read aloud *Home — II* and any other recent work. When offering feedback, first say what moves you. As you gain experience in listening empathetically, you may hear a writer's intention even if it isn't yet fully realized in the writing. One way to skillfully offer feedback is to begin by saying what genuinely moves you, then, putting your insight in the form of a question, ask the writer if you're right about his or her intention. If you're right, the writer will be grateful and open to your thoughts about how to express intention more clearly. If you're wrong, the writer will know intention is not yet clearly expressed in the writing. In either case your generous, non-judgmental attention will be meaningful to the writer, and your insights will help with your own work.

Quality of writing relates directly to quality of listening. For playwrights, as for performers and audiences, for everyone passionate about the art of theater, being an open and generous listener is paramount. Don't allow preconceptions to impede the clarity of your hearing. Using the techniques of *Overheard Voices* cultivates discriminating, non-judgmental listening. Listen to rhythm and tone in the voices around you and in the voices of your characters. "Listen" in the same way with your eyes and other senses: have no preconceptions about what they mean and notice body language, texture, shape, color, and detail.

Many playwrights write at least one play about home. If you are inspired to do so, continue *Home — II* on your own. Title it with your "What," your image of the home you have chosen.

You don't need to plan everything that will happen, but know "Who" the characters are and have a sense of the direction in which they are heading.

Before writing a new scene, first pick a date and time and a "Where." Decide "Who" is on or comes on stage. You may assign yourself a writing time or not, but once you start, keep writing until you reach a natural stopping point. Keep your "What" in mind. "Listen" to your characters and their conflicts.

After writing a scene you may choose to read it aloud and edit it, or you may prefer to write an entire act or play before starting to edit and rewrite. That's up to you. But don't judge or edit as you write.

IDEAS FOR NEW PLAYS

To become a good writer you must keep writing. Apart from writing plays, you might want to keep a journal, make notes, and keep newspaper articles about ideas for plays, write letters, poems, anything; but keep writing. Set aside time on a regular basis which is your time to keep writing.

If working with a group, tell them your ideas for plays. In light of what you've learned from this *Workbook*, explore ways to start working on these ideas. If working alone, you might want to mention your ideas for new plays to a trusted friend or two to hear their reactions.

CREATING A PLAY COLLABORATIVELY

Most playwrights enjoy working with others; otherwise they would choose to work in a more solitary genre, like novel writing. So always encourage yourself to bounce ideas off friends and to read work aloud to them.

In any innovative endeavor, only a few avenues of exploration will lead to something interesting. One possible way to write a play (not to every playwright's taste) is to collaborate with a group of actors, adjusting the work as you go. Creating plays in collaboration with performers is sometimes fruitful, sometimes frustrating.

A collaborative work may start with one of the participants figuratively throwing a burning question or questions into the empty space in the middle of a circle of collaborators. The creative process consists of theatrically expressing and refining those questions, through performing them, writing them, and finally sharing them with the audience. This is true for the creation of any play, but creating with actors means that words do not necessarily always come first. Each collaborative piece will have its chemistry and find its own process. In order for any group to effectively create a collaborative piece, someone must stand back from the work of the performers to keep an eye on and organize the larger picture. That "someone" is the playwright and/or the director.

The playwright may write scenes alone and bring them to the actors, write words for scenes that have been improvised, suggest new directions, refine, expand, and select scenes, and, ultimately, structure the play so it will communicate to the audience. In any theatrical endeavor, part of everyone's work is to drop egotistical concerns and focus on the work at hand. The writer and actors must have mutual respect for one another. If the writer and director are not the same person, there must be a trusting relationship between them and agreement about functions.

PLAYWRIGHT AND PRODUCTION

This *Workbook* is a jumping off place. You can proceed further with your writing in whatever direction feels exciting, joyful, or dangerous. There is no guarantee that when you do, you'll write a great play. But if you don't try, there's certainly no chance of it.

Your play is not finished when you have written the last line. You still need to refine the play and in doing so ease yourself toward production. Start with a reading. Read aloud yourself or ask friends to read. Invite a few people you respect to listen. From their emotional reactions and from your own listening, you'll learn what "works" and what does not. This leads to more editing and rewriting. (A play is not in its final literary form until after the revisions made during first major production, if then.) Having made changes in the script, hold a second reading. Someone who has heard your play read aloud is more likely to offer enthusiastic help than a large theater or an agent who receives your script in the mail (one of hundreds every year) . Perhaps someone who has heard your script read is, or wants to become, a director (or producer) and will offer to work with you. However, the most impassioned mover of your play toward production will most likely be you. No institution, however well-disposed, will do all the work for you.

Your first goal should be modest. Plays usually start with small productions and build to bigger ones. Try to obtain a workshop production for your play, or stage it modestly for a couple of nights in a friendly place. In working toward this, take the initiative. Check in with a local theater troupe. Talk with friends who might share your vision of theater. If your play concerns a particular group (young people, seniors, gay people, people of a particular religious or ethnic background), is a venue associated with that audience available (a church, community or social center, college auditorium, etc.)?

If you're lucky, you'll find a skilled, enthusiastic director to stage your play. Initiate a good working relationship with the director. The director needs to rely upon you as a prime resource, not a temperamental obstacle. For the dialogue between playwright and director to enrich the production, the two must agree on ground rules. Will casting and designer choices be by mutual consent? In rehearsal the playwright is usually free to make or not make the script changes the director suggests, while the director is free to accept or not accept the playwright's staging suggestions.

Keep in mind that the playwright's presence carries great weight and authority at rehearsals. Actors may strive to please the playwright, so at some rehearsals your absence might ease the director's task of encouraging actors to experiment. Often it works well for the playwright to attend beginning rehearsals (to hear the play read, to answer questions, and to make script changes), and then to attend later rehearsals (to see the production with fresh eyes).

What if you can't find a promising director? Contemporary wisdom states that the playwright is too close to the material to direct it. But, hey, Shakespeare, Molière, and Brecht directed their own work, presumably with some help from their friends. If you do direct your play in workshop, ask friends to assist and contribute ideas. A dramaturg, for instance, functions as a knowledgeable friend to the production, helping where needed, and giving advice about the script.

There are tried and true ways of producing a play but each production has its own chemistry. However unusual, it may even be appropriate for you to act in your own play. (This would certainly happen if you've written a solo performance piece.)

A production's success depends not only on the skills of the artists but on their attitude. If everyone's attention is focussed on doing the best possible job for the play (and not on ego aggrandizement) then the process is one of creative growth and the result is exciting theater.

Invite friends to later rehearsals and, if at all possible, hold several previews before the opening. Ultimately you'll experience your play most clearly with and through the audience. You'll learn from responses during a show and you'll make more changes.

WHY WRITE FOR THEATER?

The monetary rewards of writing for theater are rarely high. The pleasure of reading good reviews is balanced by the pain of reading bad ones. So why write for theater? It's a commitment to artistic growth, to personal transformation, to interaction with other theater artists, and to audiences. Theater, like the imagination of a child, is a space in which anything can happen.

SELECTED BIBLIOGRAPHY

Artaud, Antonin. *The Theater and Its Double.*

Beckett, Samuel. *Endgame.*

———. *Waiting for Godot.*

Brecht, Bertolt. The Exception and the Rule.

———. *The Threepenny Opera.*

Chekhov, Anton. *The Cherry Orchard.* In *Chekhov, The Major Plays*, English version by Jean-Claude van Itallie. New York: Applause Books, 1995.

———. *The Sea Gull.* In *Chekhov, The Major Plays*, English version by Jean-Claude van Itallie. New York: Applause Books, 1995.

———. *Three Sisters.* In *Chekhov, The Major Plays*, English version by Jean-Claude van Itallie. New York: Applause Books, 1995.

Ibsen, Henrik. *A Doll House.*

Ionesco, Eugene. *The Bald Soprano.*

———. *The Chairs.*

———. *The New Tenant.*

Miller, Arthur. *Death of A Salesman.*

Pinter, Harold. *The Caretaker.*

———. *The Dumb Waiter.*

Williams, Tennessee. *Cat on a Hot Tin Roof.*

SUGGESTED ADDITIONAL READING

Aristotle. *Poetics*.

Brook, Peter. *The Open Door: Thoughts on Acting and Theater*.

Churchill, Caryl. *Fen*.

Euripedes. *Medea*.

Garfield, Patricia. *Creative Dreaming*.

Genet, Jean. *The Balcony*. Grove Press.

Handke, Peter. "Offending the Audience" in *Kaspar and Other Plays*, translated by Michael Roloff. New York: Farrar, Straus and Giroux, Inc., 1969.

Kushner, Tony. *Angels in America*.

Shakespeare, William. *King Lear*.

van Itallie, Jean-Claude. *America Hurrah and Other Plays*. New York: Grove Press, 1978.

AFTERWORD

In 1940, at the start of the holocaust, I emigrated from Belgium, at the age of four, with my parents. I was raised in Great Neck, a prosperous Long Island suburb, whose antiseptically pretty streets and houses seemed devoid of signs of work, old age, disease, or death.

After taking a playwriting class as an undergraduate at Harvard, where I also directed some plays, I studied acting for a summer in New York City.

In 1960, living in Greenwich Village and hungry for uptown acceptance, I tried conforming to what I thought Broadway wanted by writing a play which got me an agent, a couple of polite rejection letters from producers, and little else.

Two years later, giving up hope that my work would ever be produced, I wrote two short plays to please myself. Created from a deeper place and influenced by Artaud, these plays are unusual in form. *War* is personal and dreamlike, a play "for two actors and a lady." *Motel* is a voice-over monologue spoken while three huge dolls write graffiti on the set, eventually destroying it. To my astonishment, *War* was produced in one of the first workshops in what was later called Off Off-Broadway. *Motel* was produced Off-Broadway too, in a loft two flights up on Second Avenue in the East Village at Ellen Stewart's Cafe LaMama. Even more amazing was that in November 1966, my trilogy of short plays including *Motel*, called *America Hurrah*, became a major Off-Broadway success. *America Hurrah* was a play both radical in form and in its politics (anti-Viet Nam), which I was sure the critics would loathe. Instead it was an overnight sensation.

The "apple-pie fifties" with their false facade wer
finally over. The moment was ripe for expressin;
onstage rage at America's thus far unacknowledgeɩ
aggression in the Viet Nam War and the suppressioɪ
of truth.

I was lucky to be in the right place at the right his
torical time both to learn my craft and to find
place to express it. In 1963, living on Christophe
Street (and earning my living through odd jobs in
cluding writing for "public affairs" television),
found myself part of a new, small but exciting the
ater movement. Our loose community was com
prised of mostly young people living in the Villagɩ
who had in common a disaffection with establish
ment values, a passion for making theater, and ;
yearning for a stage on which to express truths wɩ
were just discovering. We were helped by Elleɪ
Stewart who founded Cafe LaMama, produced neʋ
plays without money, and encouraged my playwrit
ing more than anyone. Our community also in
cluded director Joe Chaikin, who founded the Opeɪ
Theater (a changing ensemble of dedicated, unpaiɩ
actors) and whose partner I became in developinɡ
new theatrical forms, ultimately creating our firs
ensemble play, *The Serpent*. Al Carmines, Mariɪ
Irene Fornes, William G. Hoffman, Adriennɩ
Kennedy, Charles Ludlam, Judith Malina, Rober
Patrick, Sam Shepard, Megan Terry, Michael Smith
Robert Wilson, and Lanford Wilson were also par
of the Off Off-Broadway movement.

Theater seems always to be in urgent dialogue witl
the forces shaping the historical time. Our genera
tion discovered that words can be vehicles for lies
We came to distrust the words spoken by politicians
advertisers, preachers, journalists, and nearlʏ
everyone in power. Yet as playwright for an idealis
tic theater ensemble, it was my job to use thosɩ
same mistrusted words to tell the truth as best
could. I learned to be economical with words spo

ken onstage, to choose them carefully, and value them as anchors for feeling.

If the sixties was a decade of inspired group action, the seventies was one of retrenchment, politically and theatrically. While continuing to write plays in new theatrical forms and to teach playwriting (at Yale, Princeton, and other schools), I also began to explore and learn from past great masters of the art.

The McCarter Theater at Princeton commissioned me to write a new English version of Chekhov's *The Sea Gull*, which was later produced at the Manhattan Theater Club. The Public Theater in New York then asked me to write a new English version of *The Cherry Orchard*, which was produced at the Vivian Beaumont Theater at Lincoln Center. Later I worked on *Three Sisters* and *Uncle Vanya* for productions at the Manhattan Theater Club and Cafe LaMama in New York and the American Repertory Theater in Cambridge, Massachusetts.

In these texts I focussed on the spoken rather than the written word, working with assistants who were actors. My goal was to render Chekhov in an English neither overly contemporary nor fusty with age, a language that would flow from the actors' mouths in such a natural rhythm that adaptation from another language would not be evident.

I also wrote new versions of Euripedes, translated Ionesco and Genet from French, and directed Shakespeare. In this active study of great playwrights I proceeded like an actor, in an imaginative sense "becoming" each playwright in order to learn experientially. Some of the games in this *Workbook* derive from that learning.

In the eighties I found myself writing plays incor
porating new forms with what I had learned fron
the masters. As in the Open Theater in the sixties
I again examined the emotional source of word
with Joe Chaikin when he suffered a stroke and re
covered with aphasia (the inability to understand o
speak words appropriately). A person with aphasia
as a child just learning a language, fueled by th
frustrated desire to communicate, sometimes spon
taneously forces the few words they have at thei
disposal to explode ungrammatically into poetr}
My play *The Traveller* is about an ambitious com
poser who has a stroke during heart surgery, de
scends into a surrealistic emotional underworld
and, then, recovering some language, surfaces int
a more Chekhovian reality of family and friends
Another play, *Ancient Boys*, also based on the life o
a friend, focuses on AIDS and the suicide of an in
spired gay artist. *Bag Lady, Sunset Freeway*, an
Struck Dumb are monologues each written with ;
particular actor in mind.

Plays, of course, are fed and transformed by per
sonal development of all kinds. In 1968, I met th
Tibetan Buddhist teacher Chogyam Trungpa, Rin
poche. I used aspects of that meeting in a mono
logue in *King of the United States*, and in the eightie
wrote a play based on *The Tibetan Book of the Dea*
(transforming an ancient Eastern text into a play
using techniques developed when I wrote *The Ser
pent*). In the nineties that play, *The Tibetan Book o
the Dead*, became an opera.

As I write this manual, it feels odd to know I won'
be present when the writing games, developed ove
twenty-five years of teaching, are played. I'd like t
listen to them read back.

CHEKHOV:
THE MAJOR PLAYS

English versions by
Jean-Claude van Itallie

The Cherry Orchard
"A CLASSIC RESTORED TO THE HAND, MIND AND BLOOD OF THE CREATOR."

—The New York Times

The Seagull
"SUBLIMELY UNDERSTOOD CHEKHOV ...ABSOLUTELY TRUE TO THE ORIGINAL"

—The New York Post

Three Sisters
"CAPTURES CHEKHOV'S EXUBERANCE, MUSIC AND COMPLEXITY" *—The Village Voice*

Uncle Vanya
"THE CRISPEST AND MOST POWERFUL VERSION EXTANT." *—The New Republic*

Paper•ISBN 1-55783-162-9 • $7.95

THE LIFE OF THE DRAMA
by Eric Bentley

". . . Eric Bentley's radical new look at the grammar of
theatre . . . is a work of exceptional virtue, and readers who
find more in it to disagree with than I do will still, I think,
want to call it central, indispensable . . . The book justifies
its title by being precisely about the ways in which life
manifests itself in the theatre. If you see any crucial
interest in such topics as the death of Cordelia, Godot's
non-arrival . . . This is a book to be read and read again."

— Frank Kermode
THE NEW YORK REVIEW OF BOOKS

"The Life of the Drama . . . is a remarkable exploration
of the roots and bases of dramatic art, the most far reaching
and revelatory we have had."

— Richard Gilman
BOOK WEEK

"The Life of the Drama is Eric Bentley's magnum opus
or the put it more modestly his best book. I might call it an
aesthetic of the drama, but this again sounds ponderous;
the book is eminently lucid and often helpfully
epigrammatic. Everyone genuinely interested in the theatre
should read it. It is full of remarkable insights into many of
the most important plays ever written."

— Harold Clurman

paper • ISBN: 1-55783-110-6 • $12.95